The Quest for Excellence

THE CHASE FOR SELF-MASTERY
AND LEADERSHIP DISTINCTION

Bob McCurdy

Archway Publishing books may be ordered through booksellers or by contacting:

Archway Publishing
1663 Liberty Drive
Bloomington, IN 47403
www.archwaypublishing.com
844-669-3957

ISBN: 978-1-6657-0277-5 (sc)
ISBN: 978-1-6657-0279-9 (hc)
ISBN: 978-1-6657-0278-2 (e)

Library of Congress Control Number: 2021902834

Print information available on the last page.

Archway Publishing rev. date: 8/11/2021

CONTENTS

FOREWORD

It was July 1969, and I had just turned fifteen. As I was sitting on the curb outside Smithtown High School waiting for our summer league basketball game to begin, one of my teammates came running up to me and said Deer Park was playing, and the second half was about to begin. We all ran inside to watch. Deer Park was a good high school team, but that wasn't the reason we all wanted to watch them play. The reason was the best player on Long Island played for Deer Park. His name was Bob McCurdy. I remember watching his graceful style of play and seemingly effortless ability to score. At that time, he was the best basketball player I ever saw play this close up. I sat and watched the second half in awe.

It's now fifty years later, and we remain close friends trying to navigate life's challenges coming at us from all angles. I have always admired Bob's determination and New York grit—constantly looking for the next edge or self-improvement opportunity. Whether studying vocabulary as a teenager on the sands of Fire Island beach or having a twenty-year regular lunch date with legendary UCLA basketball coach John Wooden, Bob continued to search for knowledge and self-betterment.

The Quest for Excellence is not just a trip down memory lane for me but a reminder of what it takes to be a leader, teacher, and innovator in life and in business.

—Mitch Kupchak
President of basketball operations and general manager/Charlotte Hornets

PREFACE

I would be thrilled if those reading this book expanded and improved upon the philosophies on the following pages. Gurus—and wannabe gurus—are writing books about leadership, culture, and sales faster than you can read them. It has taken me sixty-eight years to write this one. I am not a guru; I am not famous or wildly wealthy. I am just someone who has experienced some modicum of success in sports and in business by embracing the following lessons learned along the way.

I recall reading somewhere that the only things in life you really can "keep" are the things you can "give away." So, I am hoping via this book to "give away" a few insights from the past seven decades that might serve you well.

The following pages will provide some insight as to how I built, motivated, managed, led, and acculturated the teams or companies I have been part of over the past four decades. To obtain any meaningful "stretch" goal requires that each member of the team be focused and committed to the same objective, pursuing them collectively and individually with equal zeal. I think I was reasonably successful in accomplishing this.

This leads to a phrase that I "borrowed" from basketball coach Pat Riley, a "definiteness of purpose."—Everyone knowing where they are going what the goal is, and rowing in the same direction. Achieving this and maintaining this "definiteness of purpose" is more difficult than it sounds but when it's accomplished spectacular performance usually follows.

There will be basketball references and basketball quotes throughout; I have tried to keep them to a minimum, maybe not so successfully at times.

One thing that struck me while reviewing my communication to the various companies and sales teams over the years is that many of the same issues and subjects from the 1980s are the same ones I wrote about in 2020. I guess that is why the fundamentals remain the fundamentals. The technology to execute them has certainly evolved and in many cases made them easier to execute, but the fundamentals themselves have remained largely unchanged.

Problems with fundamentals usually arise when our attention and commitment to them wanes. Just as great sports team execute them, game after game, year after year, the great performers in business do the same. There is simply no getting around this fact.

In business, we often make the simple complicated, but success in business is still largely about the fundamental daily blocking and tackling that many end up finding boring and ultimately beneath them. There is genius in the fundamentals, and high-performing companies today as in previous years remain manically committed to them.

Feel free to swipe anything that follows. It has often been said that one can never tell where a teacher's influence ends. The same is true with leaders. As leaders, we are teachers, and as with teachers, you can never tell where an effective leader's influence ends. That makes for an amazing legacy.

While I have never run a company as large as IBM, Apple, or Microsoft, the DNA of smaller companies and larger ones is strikingly similar, as is the leadership required to lead them. My experience is entirely in advertising and marketing, and as far as I have been able to tell from everyone I have spoken to, success in one industry largely parallels others.

We are the sum total of our life experience, but the core learning experiences and beliefs established early in both life and business tend to have the greatest impact on who and what kind of business executive we become. Therefore, our parents and our first bosses have an outsized impact on our lives and careers. For this reason, I have always told my children to choose their first boss very carefully.

What follows are the defining lessons that have served me well throughout my life and in business.

My accomplishments are what they are at this point due to these lessons and my earnest attempt to be true to them. I am comfortable with that.

Enjoy!

CHAPTER 1

You Can't Do It Alone

Getting a mentor is a shortcut to success.

—Bo Sanchez,
entrepreneur

I was extremely lucky throughout my career as I had some tremendous mentors. When I first got into radio in 1976, my first general manager, John Piccirillo at WLEE AM in Richmond and later at WNDE/WFBQ in Indianapolis was a visionary who had us using sales tools in the 1970s that are not as widespread as they should be even today. He was a man of principle who treated all under his employ equally. I learned a tremendous amount about life, business, and leadership from John. Denny Rossman, my first general sales manager, also played a major role in my development. Denny was a rough-and-tumble fellow from Pennsylvania who possessed a tremendous amount of street smarts.

When I joined Katz in 1980, I had the good fortune of learning and working with three outstanding leaders: Bob McArthur, Ken Swetz, and Dick Romanick.

Bob McArthur, my manager in Chicago, was smart as a whip and a wonderfully balanced man, a great role model for life and business. I valued the time I spent with Bob very much. Ken Swetz, the Katz CEO, was a military policeman. Ken was a man of intense pride and principle. Another role model at Katz in my early years was Dick Romanick, Katz's general sales manager, who oversaw all offices. Dick was a smart man with whom you did not want to mess. Dick was a big man with an intimidating glare, but he cared about his people, was smart as hell, would not accept anything but your best, and, unbeknownst too many, had a softer side. I learned a ton from Dick. He was the reason I ended up at Katz, as we hit it off on my interview. Dick knew I was interviewing with Katz's competition as well, and his last question to me was, "What are you going to do if I don't hire you?" My reply was somewhat brazen, stating, "I would come back to kick your ass and your team's asses on the streets." Not your standard response in a job interview. Luckily, he was not offended.

To describe my leadership style as somewhat authoritarian early in my management career at Katz would be accurate in part due to Romanick's influence and in part due to the team I was leading. Things needed to be either black or white in those early days as many of the salespeople I hired were individuals who had little to no sales experience. The fact that we happened to be in New York, the company's home office, did not make things easier for a young manager. As I soon understood, one's leadership and management style are determined by the capabilities of those you are responsible for leading. As my team developed, my leadership style evolved, but importantly my expectations did not.

Finally, at Katz, I had the great fortune of next working for a man named Stu Olds, a prince of a man—a giant in the radio industry and a terrific, loyal friend. Stu was probably the smartest individual that I ever encountered in business. Not only was Stu incredibly intelligent; he had a wonderful way of dealing with people and bringing teams together. All people—employees, clients, and even competitors—loved the man. When Stu transferred from Chicago to run the Detroit office, I replaced him. I soon grew weary of hearing from our clients and his agencies how terrific he was and how much they missed the man.

We both transferred to New York within months of each other in 1984 with Stu running the Katz Radio network department and me the New York sales staff. A close bond resulted. Stu assisted greatly in my evolution as a leader.

We complemented each other nicely in those early years when he became the president of Katz, and I was the general sales manager. He was the good cop, and I was the muscle—the enforcer. When he was promoted, and I replaced him as the president of Katz Radio, I soon realized that my management and leadership style that served me well as a general sales manager would not serve me quite as well as president. Thankfully, the opportunity to have observed and learned from Stu the previous four years was a master's degree in management and leadership. The lessons I learned from him served me well throughout the years. We worked with each other for over twenty-five years. He was simply the best.

One habit I developed early in my career was to read voraciously about radio, advertising, or marketing, to highlight what I read, and then to take notes from the highlighted material for easy review. On the weekends, I would drive up to the Purdue and Indiana University libraries to Xerox marketing and advertising research publications that I could not afford. I must have gone through a thousand highlighters over the years. I should have bought stock in those companies.

We forget most of what we read shortly after we have read it, and I wanted to make sure I retained the important stuff and had it handy for easy review and reference. This habit stuck with me until my recent retirement. I have kept many of these notes from the past forty years and have referred to them when needed. I have always made it a habit to devour everything about the radio business, marketing, advertising, management, and leadership, learning from people far smarter and more accomplished than I surely was.

Berkshire Hathaway's Charlie Munger said this about reading: "Develop into a lifelong self-learner through voracious reading; cultivate curiosity and strive to become a little wiser every day." No wonder he is worth billions. I simply borrowed and massaged the best thinking and ideas from the best thinkers and performers until they morphed into my own.

Many of the thoughts that follow are a mixture of the best thinking from smart people as well as my personal experience. It has been said that good artists borrow and great ones steal; I have borrowed more than my fair share and have always tried to repackage and build upon them in a manner that works for me. Throughout the years, I have never lost sight of the fact that I can learn from everybody. Not a bad thing to remember.

I have surely made numerous management and leadership mistakes over the years—mistakes that I now cringe when recalling and laugh about when reminiscing with others, but that's all part of the growth process. If you can't look back and wince a little and chuckle at some of the decisions you made or things you said, then you probably haven't grown much.

CHAPTER 2

A Great Role Model Helps

*My father didn't tell me how to live; he
lived and let me watch him do it.*

—Unknown

Hard work, dedication, sacrifice, and focus contributed greatly
to my success in sports and business. Sports-wise it was
attaining a college basketball scholarship, becoming the NCAA
Division 1's leading scorer, selected as an Associated Press and
Helms Foundation All-American, and drafted by the Milwaukee
Bucks. On the business front, it was running a number of companies
while positively influencing many in the process.

In 1976 a book titled *The Great and the Near Great: a Century of
Sports in Virginia* was published that focused on the best Virginia
athletes from the past one hundred years. I made the book, but I
would clearly fall within the latter group, the near great. I had the
privilege of playing with two truly "great" players in my college
career—Barry Parkhill at the University of Virginia, who was a
bona fide All-American; and Aron Stewart at Richmond, who twice
was a top five scorer in the United States and two-time player of
the year in our conference. Both these individuals clearly qualified
as being "great."

The one particular "skill" that enabled me to succeed in sports and business more than anything else was discipline. Interestingly, discipline is rarely perceived as being a "skill." Discipline has enabled me to pursue goals on and off the court with a single-minded determination. In the end, I guess I was blessed with the discipline of self-discipline.

Some personal background. My father, Bill McCurdy, was tall but never played sports. My mother was a wonderful woman but passed away when I was fourteen. My dad always told my brothers and me that the reason he encouraged us to play sports was to learn the importance of discipline and dedication. He was less concerned with sports excellence and more interested in excellence in anything, be it the guitar, rock polishing, etc. Discipline and the pursuit of some goal were extremely important to him, which then became important to us. No one aimlessly "drifted" at the McCurdy household.

He always made sure some goal pursuit was mixed in with the fun part of our childhood. Before we went to the beach or on a hike or whatever, we had to do something "productive." It was not out of the ordinary for us to be on the baseball field for several hours or pitching in the backyard early in the morning on the weekends before heading to the shore. He would be there encouraging, coaxing, and challenging us while he did everything that he expected us to be doing. The man was in good shape.

Dad was ahead of his time. During the winter months he had us practicing "pitching" and "foul shooting" in the living room using *Psycho-Cybernetics* techniques, which is not actually shooting or pitching but practicing form and visualizing the shot or pitch. Back then, we thought he was crazy. I have often used this concept in business. Whenever I had to give an important talk, presentation, or speech, I always tried to "experience" the venue first so I could visualize myself performing in it before I actually had to. It always took some of the nervous edge off. I recommend it to all.

Dad would get home from Manhattan around six thirty in the

evening, change into some old clothes, and before he even sat down to eat he'd have us in the back yard catching as we pitched or he'd be pitching to us at the ball field to work on our hitting. As we got older and needed sixty feet between the pitching rubber and home plate, we moved our pitching sessions to the street where we would often knock down thirty minutes of practice in the morning before he headed to the train and us to school. He clearly led by example and was a terrific role model.

He was also a bit of a weekend psychologist. I can still recall us driving by the basketball courts in an adjoining town on our way to my grandparent's house. The basketball courts were always teeming with kids playing hoops, and inevitably Dad would make some crack about those kids were the kids who were going to "make it" because they practiced more, wanted it more, and were hungrier. I invariably responded that if you didn't have us going to Grandpa's house, we'd be able to be out there too. Nonetheless, his mind games worked and served to motivate us.

CHAPTER 3

The Formative Years

It is better to look back on life and say,
"I can't believe I did that." Than to look
back and say, "I wish I did that."

—Unknown

What follows are my "baker's dozen" early life lessons that laid the foundation for my later business accomplishments while growing up in Deer Park, Long Island.

Life Lesson #1

The one who outworks the other usually wins.

There will be obstacles. There will be
doubters. There will be mistakes. But
with hard work, there are no limits.

—Michael Phelps,
Olympic swimmer

Practice might not make perfect, but those who practice and put in the time and effort stand a better chance at succeeding than those who do not. It is a simple equation. If two people are equally skilled, the one who spends the most time pursuing a goal will come out on top. This fact was instilled in me throughout my childhood. I am not sure where my dad got it, but he was a fanatic about practice and proper preparation. It rubbed off on me:

From the *University of Richmond Collegian* circa 1975:

> I can think of no one who so richly deserves success, as does McCurdy. Few athletes possess his desire or dedication. Basketball practice starts at 3:45, yet he has been found shooting as early as 1:30 each day.

Excerpt from the book *The Miracle of St. Anthony's*:

> "Looking back now it was a remarkable feat," said Kevin Eastman, Richmond's point guard and now a Boston Celtics assistant coach. "He couldn't jump that high. He couldn't run real fast. He was a prime example of how will, enthusiasm and effort allowed him to rise to another level."
>
> Eastman used to marvel at the single-minded nature of his teammate.

I always told Kevin I thought he was a bit too harsh when it came to my running and jumping ability.

Life Lesson #2

Never give up. It is not over until it is over.

It's hard to beat a person who never gives up.
—Babe Ruth,
Baseball Hall of Famer

When I was about nine years old, we were shooting a BB gun in the garage at some targets, one of which was a lit candle. An adult neighbor walked over and said he would give me $10 if I could shoot the flame off that candle from about twenty feet with one hundred shots. If I didn't, I'd owe him $5. I took the bet. The crowd surrounding the garage soon grew when after ninety-nine shots the flame was still flickering. One shot left or be out $5, which was big dough for a nine-year-old in 1961. I took the one hundredth shot, and the flame disappeared. As crazy as it might sound, that "never give up" lesson has stuck with me my entire life. I am hoping for the same thing to happen with my cancer challenge.

Life Lesson #3

If you are not improving, someone else is.

Excellence is the gradual result of always striving to do better.
—Pat Riley,
Hall of Fame basketball coach

Each of us has the same 1,440 minutes in a day, and there is only one per customer with no mulligans. The individual who allocates them more wisely in pursuit of a goal will more likely achieve that goal versus someone who doesn't. Simply maintaining the same skills is not enough to withstand the competitive challenge of someone or some company that wants "it" more and continues to progress and improve. Sports is competitive. Life is competitive. Business is competitive. Just as relationships are getting better or worse, the same is true when it comes to our professional skills; never do they stay the same. The one who wants it more usually gets it.

Life Lesson #4

Politics in life is a reality. Get used to it.

Life is not fair; get used to it.
—Bill Gates,
cofounder Microsoft

In spite of all the practice and time spent on the ball field as a youngster, I can still recall the disappointment I experienced when my Little League coach's son made the all-star team and I did not, and in my mind I was clearly the better player. I voiced this to my dad, and he agreed, but his response was simple: life was not always fair; get over it, and do something about it. He said that you will experience perceived injustices throughout life and encouraged me to work harder, so that next year I would be the obvious choice for the team. I followed his advice, and the next year I was the obvious choice. The lesson was a simple one, but it stuck; be considerably better than the competition; if you are not, you will never control your own destiny.

Life Lesson #5

Good things happen to those who pay the price.

*I'm a great believer in luck, and I find the
harder I work the more I have of it.*
—Thomas Jefferson

I recall reading an article in the newspaper the summer between my freshman and sophomore year in high school about a great Long Island high school basketball player, Tom Riker, that changed my life. The article contained a picture of Tom and detailed all the colleges wooing him for his hoop services. Prior to reading the article, I practiced when it was convenient or when another kid would join me at the court. Being on the court alone and practicing by oneself was lonely, and it was hot in the summer. After reading the article, I said to myself, "If he could do it, so could I." I redoubled my practice regimen and spent hours at an elementary school refining my basketball skills to the point where, like Riker, dozens of colleges were competing for my services several years later. I figured out once that in a seven-year period, I had spent one full year of my life on the basketball court—every minute of every hour of every day of every month for one full year—a pretty solid commitment. This cemented forever in my mind that success above all is a personal choice. A choice of determining what you are willing to give up in pursuit of certain goals.

Life Lesson #6

Don't be derailed from pursuing your dreams.

*Don't give up on your dreams, or your
dreams will give up on you.*
—John Wooden,
Hall of Fame basketball coach

In sports, life, or business, things don't always work out the way we'd like. After an outstanding freshman season on the court at the University of Virginia, my sophomore year was one to forget. The coach that recruited me went to coach at Notre Dame with Digger Phelps, and a new coach who was hired emphasized defense, not offense. Anyone who ever saw me play would understand that defense was not my strong suit. The Hall of Fame basketball player Adrian Dantley once said, "You don't make All American playing defense." I probably took him too literally. Additionally, I was injured in preseason, fell behind the others, and didn't receive the playing time I thought I deserved. After being widely thought of as a likely starter my sophomore year, I was mired on the bench and miserable to the point where my GPA tumbled as much as my scoring average.

I can recall a conversation with my father in the stands at Madison Square Garden after a very disappointing loss to Lafayette College in the NIT. We discussed whether I stay at UVA or transfer elsewhere to play. Caught up in the disappointment, I told him I had made up my mind, and I was I was going to stay—that I had many friends at the school and that I was content being just "another player." His response was measured but resonated. He stressed that it was certainly my choice but that I should be careful to never lose sight of my dreams, never let someone else stand in the way of achieving them, and moving forward, if I decided to stay at UVA, to not complain about what you permitted.

Thankfully, I transferred to the University of Richmond, and things worked out perfectly. Good advice, Pop. Following my dream and transferring to Richmond changed the entire trajectory of my life in so many ways.

Life Lesson #7

You better hustle.

Without hustle, talent will only carry you so far.
—Gary Vaynerchuk,
entrepreneur/author

The second game of the season my senior year against Cal State Fullerton, I missed a couple of easy shots and let it affect my play; in other words, I was not only playing poorly but worst of all not hustling. My coach at Richmond, Carl Slone, noticed this and yanked me out of the game, sitting me on the bench for extended minutes. We ended up losing the game by four points, a game we should have easily won, largely due to my poor play and prima donna attitude.

The newspapers piled on as well, writing in advance of our next game, "And if Bob McCurdy and Eric Gray loaf the way they did Thursday night in the first half, this coming game could be a mismatch in Furman's favor. Slone will find out tonight if his disciplinary action will inspire McCurdy and Gray to play with more enthusiasm."

The message he communicated came through loud and clear—it is a privilege to be allowed to compete, nobody is indispensable, don't become your own worst enemy, and you better hustle or else. It was a lesson I would never forget. Always give 100 percent. Thanks, Coach Slone. I needed that.

Life Lesson #8

Failure to prepare is preparing to fail.

I will prepare and someday my chance will come.
—Abraham Lincoln

At Richmond, besides my brother who also played on the team, my closest pal was a player named Kevin Eastman who possessed the same drive as I did, embracing the importance of practice and controlling what you can control. We figured out ways to sneak into the gym and used a clothes hanger to turn on the lights to practice our shooting until our fingers bled. And when they did bleed, we just put band-aids on them and kept shooting. It didn't matter if we had just returned from a road trip or if it was hours before practice; we were in the gym, and I credit him for much of my success on the basketball court as without him as our point guard, I would likely not have accomplished what I did. Kevin went on to a great college and professional coaching career with the Celtics for years with Doc Rivers, winning an NBA championship, then with the Clippers in Los Angeles. He is a terrific motivational speaker and has written an outstanding book titled *Why the Best Are the Best*. We practiced hard so we would be prepared.

Life Lesson #9

Well done is better than well said.

It is good to be a good doer than a good talker.
—Benjamin Franklin

Another lesson that year stands out occurred later my senior year. After a game with the Citadel, one of the weaker teams on our schedule, I had gotten into early foul trouble, received a technical foul, and sat a good part of the game, which thankfully we won. I ended up with twenty-five points in twenty-four minutes. At this point of the season, I was in the national scoring race with two great players, Adrian Dantley of Notre Dame and David Thompson of North Carolina State, so twenty-five was not a particularly strong game.

I recall having dinner after the game and my dad asked how I thought I played. He only made it to a couple of games each year, so I was disappointed not to have played better. I replied something like, "Okay. I had twenty-five, but everyone there knew I could have had forty." His response still rings in my ears. He simply said, "How would they know if you didn't do it?" The next time we played, we trounced them, and I had thirty-one points by halftime. Well done is always better than well said. Les Robinson, the Citadel coach at the time, said recently in an article, "We played a box-and-one against him and tried a lot of other defensive things but the guy could just score."

Life Lesson #10

Suck it up, and know when to keep your mouth shut.

Don't let your tongue cut your throat.
—Irish proverb

After both my junior and senior seasons in college, my right leg, due to an Achilles tendon injury, was in a cast for six to eight weeks. My senior season it was the norm to get a cortisone shot each week to enable me to play. I was lucky to have finished my senior season, as there were games that I was not sure I could suit up. The injury was not good timing for the upcoming NBA draft when various college all-star games take place, which due to the injury I had to decline. My dad had several high-level contacts in the NBA who called around to the teams canvassing interest in me with the feedback being that I'd be drafted in the second to fourth round, which back then with fewer teams was pretty good.

When draft day came and my family and I were all sitting in the backyard waiting for my agent's phone call, which came far later than expected, I went in a lower round drafted by the Milwaukee Bucks who had just traded Kareem Abdul-Jabbar to the Lakers for a slew of young forwards, which happened to be my position. It was the biggest disappointment in my life up until that point. The Richmond papers called my house asking for a quote, and I blasted the NBA for being "clueless," not a smart thing to say to a potential future employer. The next day in the Richmond paper the headline was, "The NBA Doesn't Like McCurdy, McCurdy Doesn't Like The NBA." The article contained an all-time dumb quote: "Some of these guys they drafted ahead of me … it's ridiculous." I can still see the expression on my father's face when he read the paper. It was his "How dumb can you get?" face. The moral: do not let your tongue cut your throat.

Life Lesson #11

Disappointment is part of life. Deal with it.

Life isn't fair. It's true, and you still
have to deal with it. Learning to rise
above it is the ultimate reward.

—Harvey MacKay,
author

I chose not to pursue the Bucks but instead chose to pursue an overseas option due to a much friendlier schedule (i.e., far fewer games than the NBA; additionally it was more money).

The day before I was to fly to Chicago to meet with the representatives from an Italian team, I again injured my Achilles tendon in a pickup game with my brother and a couple of other players and was unable to make the trip. It was the end of basketball for me. I had seen too many ex-college athletes hold on to the "dream" for too long and always vowed I would not be one of them, plus the money back then was a fraction of what it is today. It was time to pursue a career outside basketball.

Life Lesson #12

Ready or not, here I come.

> *Nothing is predestined. The obstacles*
> *of your past can become the gateways*
> *that lead to new beginnings.*
>
> —Ralph Blum,
> cultural anthropologist

While the dream of playing professional basketball never materialized due to the tendon injury, I was unprepared for the business world.

The following is taken from the November 20, 1989, *Sports Illustrated* article titled "The Lost Generation," which focused on all the nation's leading scorers who never made it professionally. It quoted me accurately:

> Not playing in the NBA helped me in business because psychologically I still had something to

prove. And in sales you vent competitive energy every day. Suddenly the gym rat who had cut classes to shoot hoops realized his English degree was of little use. I was almost incoherent when I got out of college. Here I was hoping to be a businessman and I couldn't even talk basketball.

In retrospect, I wish I had used a different word than *incoherent*. I was bad but not that bad; I could speak. It is amazing I was even in the article in the first place as I had been refusing the *Sports Illustrated* writer's phone calls as I thought it was a prank being hatched by one of my salespeople.

When you are on a college athletic scholarship, you get used to people doing things for you that the average student doesn't experience. Now I had to take care of myself and do what everyone else had to do. I quickly called upon my childhood lessons regarding hard work and discipline and brought them to the work force, although it was far from an easy transition. It just had never occurred to me that after college I would not be playing basketball somewhere for at least a couple of years.

I took stock of what I needed to do to improve and bought every Dale Carnegie book ever published as well as the book that I still have to this day: *Thirty Days to A More Powerful Vocabulary*. I carried that book everywhere. I recall being at the beach with high school friend Mitch Kupchak, the great University of North Carolina power forward, Olympic gold medal winner, NBA player, and NBA general manager. He asked why I was reading a vocabulary book while there were so many girls to impress sitting around us. I told him that he had a nice pro contract waiting for him and could afford to focus on the women but that I, on the other hand, needed to find a job and jumpstart a career—an impressive display of focus on my part.

The job search was rocky. I had no clue what I wanted to do, and

I truly could have been the worst interviewer in the history of the US workforce. I mean I was bad. Nervous, sweating, everything. I have shared this fact with numerous individuals I interviewed over the years. In fact, due to my ineptitude interviewing in those early years, I always had a soft spot in my heart for job candidates who did not interview well, often allowing them to come back and give it another shot.

I believed then and I do now that it was wise to look beyond interviewing skills, as the nervousness exhibited could have been due to them wanting the job so badly, as was the case with me. Many of my best hires over the years turned out to be the individuals who would never have made it to the interviewing hall of fame.

Life Lesson #13

What doesn't kill you makes you stronger.

*Only door-to-door salesmen know
it is a hard "knock" life.*

—Unknown

Upon graduation from college, financial support was not forthcoming from home. During my job search, I ended up living in a boarding house surrounded by men who had too much of an affinity for cheap wine and were allergic to work.

Thankfully, I landed a job at Mid-Atlantic Industries in Richmond, selling Norelco dictating machines to businesses door-to-door. Yep, door-to-door. I moved out of the boarding house and into an apartment complex surrounded by the cafeteria workers who had been serving me meals the past several years at Richmond. The living arrangements were not great, but it was better than a boarding house, and at $90 a month it was at least affordable. I was in heaven until I hit the streets and discovered how difficult the product was going to be to sell. On top of that, I had to go to the apartment next door with rifle in hand to stop a man from beating his wife. I was missing hoops more every day.

Door-to-door sales was not easy. It did three things, though: it toughened me up, taught me to think on my feet and quickly made clear exactly what I did not want to do the rest of my life. A good thing to know at a young age.

CHAPTER 4

This Is a Helluva Lot Harder than Basketball

It's usually when it is harder than you thought,
and taking longer than you thought, that
it turns out better than you thought.

—Unknown

Thankfully, my earlier life lessons prepared me for the challenges I would be facing in business. They provided me with a set of tried and true beliefs that I knew from personal experience worked and that I could fall back on when the going got tough, which it surely did. Many of the basics required to succeed in sports mirror what it takes to succeed in business—hard work, persistence, preparation, repetition, etc. The difference in business is that you don't have thousands of people cheering you on; you've got to create your own momentum, your own "wind." What follows are my business life-altering experiences:

Business Lesson #1

Good luck must be earned.

Today I will do what others won't, so tomorrow
I can accomplish what others can't.

—Jerry Rice,
Hall of Fame football player

Thankfully, a radio station in Richmond—WLEE AM—which I had called on in an attempt to sell dictating equipment, had a general manager who thought I might have some potential buried deep, deep inside. He told me to stay with this door-to-door sales job and see him in six months when I had some experience. I stayed in touch with him, keeping him apprised of my progress.

Before going back, I had gotten my hands on some "radio" information and recorded it on a dictating machine, which I listened to over and over for several weeks prior to meeting with him again. When I went back in six months with some sales experience under my belt and some radio knowledge to boot, God bless him, he hired me. Both he and his general sales manager were outstanding role models and mentors. I was extremely fortunate to have started my radio career with these two individuals. They both had a hugely positive impact on my life.

Adios, Norelco.

Business Lesson #2

Outwork your boss.

One key to success is to have lunch at the
time of day most people have breakfast.
—Robert Breault,
American operatic tenor

The first day on the job at WLEE, I made it a point to get to the radio station early so I would be the first one in and make a good first impression. To my surprise, the general manager was already there. He was married and had four kids, and I was single, with none. He greeted me at the door with a smile and said, "Good afternoon." It was the last time I let him get to the office before me. No one, particularly my boss, an individual who was already quite successful, was going to outwork me. After all, my work ethic was within my control. I made sure he saw my car in the parking lot when he got to the office every day thereafter.

Business Lesson #3

The importance of practice, drilling, and rehearsing.

People asked why I practiced so much. The
answer was simple: I was not going to let someone
with more natural ability be better than me.
—Unknown

My PDR habit from sports translated nicely to business. I'd go home from the radio station, get a quick dinner, and then head back to the station with a couple of beers, one for me and one for the evening jock, to practice my "pitch," study, learn more about the industry, and get ready for the next day so I could hit the street running. It's been said that practice is a means of "inviting" the improvement desired. I was doing everything possible to "invite" it, but it did not come without some considerable coaxing.

Speaking of PDR, since 1976 I have always allocated an hour or two a day Monday through Friday, to professional study, reading, and self-improvement. Spending two hours on the train each day into Manhattan for thirty-plus years made this easy. I worked when the other commuters were sleeping. I figured if I was going to be away from my wife and kids, I might as well do something productive. On Saturday and Sunday, the number went up to three to four hours a day. I thought that with twenty-four hours a day, if I sleep for about eight, that leaves sixteen hours to squeeze three or four hours devoted to my professional growth. That still left me a dozen hours for the family, more than enough time for everyone to get tired of me.

This was an inviolate part of my routine and something that I committed myself to when I first got into business. If it were going to be a busy weekend when the kids were younger, I would get up 5:00 a.m. and knock out a few hours before they even woke up. It became a lifelong habit. I recognized you will never "find" time for anything. If you want the time, you must make it.

For the first time I will admit to something that is unknown to all but my children. It was not always easy to squeeze out three to four hours per day on the weekends with four kids under six years of age. It required some ingenuity, so in the 1980s I went out and bought the headgear that the guys used at the airports that guided the jets to the gates. I figured if it was good enough to cancel out the sound of a jet engine, it was good enough to cancel out four kids when all hell was breaking loose. I only pulled these out when my wife was out of the house shopping. The kids were jumping all over, but so long as there was no blood, all was good. I needed to "practice" my craft.

Gary Player, one of golf's legends, tells the story that he was practicing in a bunker and some fan approached just in time to see him sink a sand shot. The bystander yelled, "Fifty bucks if you do that again," and Player stepped up and holed the second shot. The guy then yelled, "Okay, $100 if you do it again." Sure enough, the third shot went in. The bystander looked on with amazement and said, "I've never seen anyone so lucky in my entire life," to which Player responded, "Well, the more I practice, the luckier I get!"

One other thing that has served me well over the years in addition to PDR was turning my home literally into my own personal "university,"—my place of study. I have always believed that those who succeeded displayed a willingness to develop themselves. I recall a Groucho Marx quote: "TV makes me smarter. Whenever someone turns it on, I go in another room and read." I always limited my tube exposure. Even television sports exposure. Why should I watch someone else pursue their profession when I could be making myself better by pursuing mine? Over time, these "found" hours added up, enabling me to become a more effective professional.

Business Lesson #4

No one turns down a request for advice.

Don't be shy about asking for help. It doesn't mean you are weak; it only means you are wise.

—Unknown

You can learn a lot if you just ask. Despite being an untested rookie in the business, I wanted to learn, so I reached out to people inside the station (jocks, our program director, and engineer), studiously observing and listening to them as well as those outside the radio station who could teach me and make me better.

One such individual was Al Pariser, who was the VP of Research at Arbitron New York in the late 1970s. I used to call him at lunch and recorded his answers to my questions (with his permission). In the evening, I went home and transcribed his responses so that nothing would be lost in translation. Here was a brilliant, established man spending thirty minutes on the phone with me—a total rookie—once a week answering my questions. I think he was happy to do so and got as much enjoyment out of it as I did knowledge. I learned a lot from Al. I still have the tapes.

I did the same thing with the VP of Research at Katz radio, a national radio sales company that, unbeknownst to me, I would join several years later and spend three decades with. Bill Schrank would spend his time on the phone answering my questions about various research topics that proved to be very helpful and enabled me to separate myself from other local sellers in town. In fact, Bill was the reason I ended up at Katz as he suggested to Dick Romanick, Katz's general sales manager, that he meet with me. Without Bill, I have no idea where I would have ended up professionally.

I kept up this habit of learning from people smarter than I. Figuring that I'd be able to position my stations more effectively to the buying community if I understood the nuances of programming more deeply, I reached out to Lee Abrams, father of the Superstars format, and did sales calls with him in Minneapolis. Jeff Pollock came and addressed my New York staff; I spoke regularly with E. Alvin Davis, a respected programming consultant who became a great mentor, and Mike Joseph, the creator of the Hot Hits format.

In the early 2000s as we began to penetrate upper-client and planning levels, I reached out to Erwin Ephron, who was a genius when it came to media. In 2003, *American Demographics Magazine* honored him as one of the five most influential media people of the last twenty-five years. Erwin became a good friend and valued mentor.

I reached out to other ad agency and industry legends like Stan Richards, David Lubars, Andrew Robertson, Alex Bogusky, David Verklin, Lee Clow, Ted Ward, Mike Hughes, Bob Liodice, Andrew Keller, and many others over the years to get their perspective on topics in which I was deficient. They all made me smarter.

Business Lesson #5

The best investment is in your own professional growth.

> *"Investing in yourself is the best investment you will ever make. It will not only improve your life, it will improve the lives of all those around you."*
> —Robin Sharma,
> Canadian writer

You can lose your job and your car keys, but you can't lose what's in your head—what you have learned. In radio, a station's audience ratings contribute greatly to the rates a station could charge an advertiser, and the ratings services that determine each station's audience are subject to the laws of statistics, as they utilize a sample to project the listening behavior of the entire population.

Since the ratings contributed to the rate/price one could charge an advertiser, and since the rates one could charge contributed to one's income, I decided I had better learn as much as I could about statistics that were influencing my income.

I called Butler University and asked for the head of its statistics department and hired him to come to the radio station after hours to tutor me one-on-one. I was not rolling in the dough, and the professor charged me $50 per hour in 1978, but it was worth it.

I had him come several times a week for about six months. The knowledge I acquired from this professor has served me well for forty-four years. Every dollar paid to him came back to me at least a hundredfold. This kind of ROI has always been the case with every nickel I spent out of my pocket to learn more about my profession.

The personal Apple 11 computer had just come out in the late 1970s, and I had just quit my job in Indianapolis at WNDE/WFBQ without having a job due to disenchantment with the new general manager. My wife, who was one of my salespeople (I do not recommend this), had quit several weeks prior due to her disenchantment with him as well, and we had recently bought a house. So, money was tight and my future uncertain. One thing I was certain about was that there were sales applications with the Apple 11 computer, and I was going to be one of the first to uncover them. I bought it and taught myself how to program and developed some helpful radio sales programs. While the computer was expensive, the printer was doubly so. I could not afford to buy it but had to lease it through my brother-in-law's company. Sounds crazy today, but back then a good printer cost more than the computer.

The Apple computer, along with Bill Shrank, played a major role in getting me hired by Katz. I lugged it to New York, Detroit, and Chicago for my Katz interviews and made a positive impression. The Katz managers thought I was a little crazy, but at least they thought I was a forward-thinking nut. An investment in yourself always pays the best interest.

Business Lesson #6

Attempt to elevate your job into an art form.

*You must dedicate your life to mastering
your skill. That's the secret to success and
is the key to being regarded honorably.*

—Jiro Ono,
Japanese chef

Elevate "interest" into "total commitment." One of the books I read years ago stated that weekdays were for keeping up with the Joneses, and the weekends were the time to get "ahead of them." I took it to heart. In fact, the blog I have been writing every Saturday morning for the past six years is titled, B.O.M. for "Better on Monday."

I recently added up all this time over the past forty-four years that I have spent on professional self-improvement, and it totaled about forty-four thousand hours, give or take a few hours. This works out to be the equivalent of twenty years of "work weeks" devoted to professional mastery. Crazy? Maybe, but I was lucky as my profession developed into my hobby, so the time spent "improving" was not forced—totally voluntary and not work. It is true that if you love what you do you never have to work a day in your life. It is also true that you do not get exceptionally good at anything without becoming somewhat obsessed with it. Day by day, you get better than you were yesterday.

My goal in both sports and business has always been to come as close as I could to achieving my potential. John Wooden had what I thought to be a terrific definition of success—defining it as, "Success is peace of mind, which is a direct result of self-satisfaction in knowing you did your best to become the best that you are capable of becoming." I have always believed one of life's greatest joys is attempting to live up to your potential. There is a purity to that pursuit. I have never fully accomplished this, but it has been a satisfying chase.

Businesses never become great by solely chasing dollars. They become great by having employees who take immense pride in their responsibilities attempting to elevate their work into something special. I have never known any great performer, regardless of profession, who had not relished the rigor of pursuing and narrowing his or her personal performance gap.

Business Lesson #7

Your word is your bond.

Integrity is choosing your thoughts and actions based on values rather than personal gain.
—Unknown

A commitment is a commitment. Winners make commitments. Losers make promises. My general manager and general sales manager, Picirrillo and Rossman, left WNDE/WFBQ. As I was not comfortable with their replacements, I began interviewing in New York and Chicago with national radio rep companies where I secured a job with Katz Radio in Chicago in 1980 for $50,000. These companies represented local radio stations to national advertising agencies across the country who were interested in reaching consumers in local markets.

In the interim, Picirrillo and Rossman were hired at another radio station in Indianapolis and offered me a position that doubled that income. This was a lot of money in 1980, but I had already accepted the Katz position and felt I could not go back on my word. So, my wife and I moved to Chicago $50,000 poorer. I felt that to back out on Katz would have been poor form no matter what the personal connection or financial gain might have been in Indianapolis. In the end as usually happens, everything worked out fine.

Business Lesson #8

Taking a step back can be smart.

One step back, two steps forward
still gets you ahead.

—Unknown

What might have appeared to be taking a step back leaving a sales management position in Indiana for a sales position in Chicago was a good move. In 1981 after a year selling in Chicago, a management position opened in Minneapolis to run the newly opened Katz office. When presented with the opportunity, I jumped at it and never looked back. In short order, my decision to move forward with Katz instead of the Indianapolis offer led to two career steps forward with a world class national sales organization providing me with a much broader view of the radio industry. This would also lead to a huge opportunity several years hence.

Business Lesson #9

A little extra hustle.

Go above-and-beyond not because anyone is
asking you to, but because you want to.

—Unknown

Back in the 1980s an industry trade, *Radio & Records*, was delivered to my office every Monday. I learned it was actually delivered on Saturday, so instead of waiting until Monday, I would throw the kids into their car seats and drive to our mailroom to pick it up Saturday so that by Monday morning I was hitting the streets smarter and better prepared than the competition. Being better on Monday has never let me down.

Business Lesson #10

Succeed or fail with like-minded individuals.

> *Show me your team, and I will*
> *show you your future.*
> —Unknown

Business is difficult enough, but to have a team that does not view things similarly makes your job doubly difficult. In 1984, I transferred to New York to manage the Katz office. This was a gamble by Dick Romanick as I was a manager in title only coming from a one-person operation in Minneapolis.

The staff I inherited was complacent and underperforming, and it quickly became apparent that the sales team needed immediate replacement.

I wanted people who wanted to make a difference regardless of their experience level, so instead of hiring overpriced "experienced" salespeople, I hired inexperienced, hungry individuals with little to no sales experience. I made sure these new hires had the right attitude and work ethic and wanted to make a name for themselves and trained the daylights out of them morning and night, Monday through Friday. It was an intense, stressful, exciting time.

If I was going to fail or succeed, I was going to do so with like-minded, dedicated people. This went against the norm, but it worked; the new guard replaced the old guard, and an entirely new culture was established.

The industry thought we were crazy going in this direction, and we were the recipient of a lot of ridicule inside and outside the company, but these newly hired and trained salespeople rose to the occasion. The following are just a few from the first couple of training programs who had terrific careers at and after Katz:

Mike Agovino—president/CEO Workhouse Connect LLC; cofounder COO Triton Digital; former CEO Clear Channel Radio Sales.

Steven Moskowitz—CEO, Centennial Holdings; former CEO NextG Networks; former U.S. president American Tower Corp.

Bob Turner—president Network Sales Azteca American Television; president D&R/Interep; president/founder Clear Channel Radio Sales/Interep.

Evan Greenberg—CEO/owner Allscope Advertising.

Erik Hellum—chief operating officer Townsquare Media.

Mark Gray—CEO/Katz Media Group.

Paul O'Malley—president Charleston Radio Group.

Gregg Wolfson—president Local Media San Diego.

Melissa Goidel—founder Heart Wired Holding Co., CRO Refinery 29 Inc.

Mike Pallad—president Modern Luxury National Portfolio; president Undertone; Apple Music director of sales.

Bill Sickles—partner lead/Google.

I wanted to make sure there was no misunderstanding as to how everyone should approach their jobs in New York, so I created the Katz Norms and Expectations in 1984. The acculturation process was now in full swing.

Norms and Expectations of the Katz Account Executive

Moses only had Ten Commandments; we had fourteen.
We are expected:

1. To communicate flawlessly with our clients.
2. To exercise solid sales fundamentals.
3. To be completely prepared for every submission. It is expected we stay until the job is finished. We must practice our pitches the way athletes practice their sport.
4. To know our client's product every bit as deeply and thoroughly as they do.
5. To compete relentlessly for every piece of business.
6. To be constantly looking for ways to improve ourselves. Your manager can not and should not do it all. Commit to improve yourself so tomorrow's opportunity will not find you lacking.
7. To be familiar with all the sales tools at your disposal. The business moves at too fast a pace for us to say, "Maybe I coulda, shoulda, woulda."
8. That everything be done in an excellent manner. Everything we do contributes to the overall Katz image. Autograph all you touch with excellence.

9. To critique ourselves each day, taking pride in what we've accomplished as well as analyzing where we can improve. Honest reflection, not rationalization.
10. To be knowledgeable about our industry as well as others.
11. To portray a professional aura in both dress and demeanor.
12. To understand that we are Katz's most important resource. When we lose a piece of business, we do not point fingers. We take a step back and formulate a strategy for the next opportunity.
13. The superior national rep of the 1980s will have working relationships with the planners, account supervisors, account execs, media director, and clients.
14. Every contact with our clients is not only an opportunity to sell ourselves; it is an opportunity to sell the Katz organization.

Business Lesson #11

One company indivisible.

*Alone we can do so little, together
we can do so much.*

—Helen Keller,
American political activist

Outstanding results are impossible without alignment. In 1986, I became general sales manager of Katz Radio overseeing all the Katz sales offices around the country. As with the New York sales management position, it was challenging being relatively young and overseeing sales managers and salespeople who were ten to twenty years older, but it contributed greatly to my growth as a manager and leader. To get all office managers aligned as to what was expected, I created the norms and expectations for Katz sales managers. While we had offices around the country, when it came to competence, expertise, and culture, we soon became one company indivisible.

Norms and Expectations of the Katz Manager

1. Communication: It is the manager's responsibility to ensure that the staff communicates to our clients in the proper manner and communicates effectively to their team.

2. We need to contact clients that appear on the first page of the Problem/Priority report each week discussing strategy, market changes, problems, and opportunities. This ensures proper communication between Katz and our clients who are experiencing revenue challenges.

3. A timely and thorough response to corporate requests is expected. We are professionals; we must respond and do business as professionals.

4. As managers, we are responsible for the performance of our offices. We set the pace, tone, and expectations of our sales team. Our norms and expectations become theirs. Are we assisting our staff's professional growth? Have we created a challenging environment that encourages excellence?

5. We must continue to grow as professionals and continue to challenge ourselves to improve daily. How are we better today than yesterday? We are Katz's most important resource; we must continue to challenge ourselves to improve. We can't improve others if we don't first improve ourselves. Everyone thinks of changing the world, but no one thinks of changing himself/herself. Improve yourself first.

6. We are responsible for the continued training of our sales staff. It is the manager's responsibility to see that salespeople

are provided with the guidance/coaching to reach their potential. As managers, we are only as good as the people who work for us. Effective managers train their replacement and have them waiting in the wings.

7. We must provide the sales staff with the feedback to improve. We want managers who are clock builders, not time tellers. Develop your people every day.

8. We must master our sales and research tools. What we expect of our sellers we must also expect of ourselves.

9. On a semiannual basis, performance evaluations are to be completed. This accomplishes several things. First, we will be giving the salesperson formal feedback and ways to improve, and it will enable us to understand the progress they either are or are not making.

10. We should always be looking to identify solid sales prospects. Interviewing should be an ongoing process. Katz can always use exceptional sales professionals.

Business Lesson #12

The skills that got you there are not enough to keep you there.

The key to success is to keep growing
in all areas of life—mental, emotional,
spiritual, as well as physical.

—Julius Erving,
Hall of Fame basketball player

In 1990, I became president of Katz Radio, replacing Stu Olds, who was an outstanding mentor. I knew the technical side of the business, but Stu taught me the more important interpersonal part of leadership. My reputation was one of a hard-charging "sales guy" who had challenging expectations. I now needed to develop somewhat of a softer side as well. Stu's assistance here was invaluable. Some who worked for me might laugh that I am even claiming of having a "softer" side.

Business Lesson #13

Be careful before you hit "send."

What do you do with a mistake: Recognize it, admit it, learn from it, forget it.
—Dean Smith,
Hall of Fame basketball coach

When I became president, computers at Katz Radio were few and far between, so I ordered one. In the meantime, I used an internal system that enabled me to type and send what I typed to myself or anyone else in the company. In this case, I was typing notes from a confidential president's meeting I had just attended, which focused on the extremely sensitive subject of the dissolution of one of our sister companies that was having difficulty getting traction. My intention was to send these notes only to myself.

My tenure as Katz president at this point was probably only two to three weeks. Well, I hit the wrong button, and my notes were sent mistakenly to the entire staff of the company being dissolved—a disaster of major proportions. I can remember being called up to Ken Swetz's office to meet with him and Stu Olds. A most unpleasant meeting. Dean Smith above says to "forget" mistakes. It was quite a while before any of us forgot this one. I was extremely happy when the computer finally arrived. Try to avoid doing this ever but particularly the first few weeks after a promotion.

Business Lesson #14

Be at your best when your best is needed.

Everything negative, pressure, challenges,
is all an opportunity for me to rise.

—Kobe Bryant,
Hall of Fame basketball player

Pyramid Broadcasting and Atlantic Ventures in Boston decided to use their combined revenue pitting the Katz Radio Group versus our arch competitor, Interep, with the winner of this "pitch off" gaining considerable revenue and momentum in the eyes of the radio industry. This was literally the equivalent of a radio showdown at the OK corral between Katz and Interep.

We had the relationship with Atlantic Ventures, and Interep had a deep relationship with Pyramid and its larger-than-life CEO, Richie Balsbaugh, with whom we had no relationship. Balsbaugh would carry more weight in the making of the final decision.

Interep presented first and very effectively did its "dance" before leaving the twenty or so executives from Atlantic Ventures and Pyramid with expensive gifts from Tiffany. That was not our style. We were to present the next day.

The word we received from our Atlantic Ventures contacts was that Interep hit it out of the park and was very impressive.

We got to Boston the night before and practiced our presentation well into the night. The next morning came, and we could tell after our first few presenters—based on body language and questions— that the room was leaning heavily Interep.

Next to present was our Christal president, Bill Fortenbaugh. This was before PowerPoint, so we had slides created that were stored in trays. As Bill's slides were being set up, the individual executing the tray exchange lost control, with the slides scattering all over the floor. Disaster. Things could not be going worse for us on such an important presentation.

I was up next and knew I needed a Hail Mary to pull this out and said to all in the room, "Buckle your seatbelts," and presented. It was a proud moment. We, the Katz Radio Group, secured the "order" before we even left the conference room that day, leaving Interep out in the cold. A big win for the company, which elevated the KRG several notches above Interep throughout the industry and really gave one of our sister companies, Eastman, a shot in the arm in terms of acquiring some outstanding new clients.

Business Lesson #15

Be proud to communicate what you stand for.

Stand tall and be proud of what you are.
Never back down from what you believe in ...
and never be ashamed of who you are.

—Unknown

No one knows if you don't tell them. It was during these Katz years that I was looking for a vehicle to communicate to our staff, our clients, and prospective clients what Katz Radio and its culture stood for as a way of separating our company from the competition. Culture is not just internal. Our culture was our brand, and I wanted it known throughout the industry. I wrote a series of booklets that communicated in writing our core values for all to see, evaluate, dispute. The content of two of these booklets is located in the "Added Value" section at the back. I have heard that many of those who received them back in the early 1990s still have them. They are surely worth reviewing.

Business Lesson #16

Always challenge yourself.

*Unless you try to do something beyond what you
have already mastered, you will never grow.*
—Ralph Waldo Emerson,
American philosopher

Find out if you are as good as you think you are. In 1996 after running Katz for six years, Stu Olds, who was then the CEO of the Katz Radio Group, which was comprised of three national radio sales companies—Katz Radio, Christal Radio, and Eastman Radio—approached me to start another national sales company as its president. I was already running the #1 company in our industry, Katz Radio, and had it firing on all cylinders, had a world class general sales manager in Mike Agovino, and a terrific management and sales staff but could not pass up the opportunity to "test" myself by starting a company from scratch. It was a leap into the unknown with considerable risk, but I always believed that if you hide from risk, you hide from its rewards. I now had to walk my talk. Thus, Sentry Radio was born.

It was an opportunity for me to see if I was as good as I thought I was or if I was a product of Katz's momentum. Some discomfort is a good thing, as revenue and personal growth are not offshoots of comfort. Also, too much professional stability can evolve into professional stagnancy.

We already had one major broadcast client for Sentry, but we needed another one. I put a full-court press on landing Bonneville Broadcasting as our second corporate client. We had done business with them in San Francisco, and they were terrific people. I took up residence in a Marriott hotel in Salt Lake City for a week and one by one met with the Bonneville general managers from around the country and convinced them to jump on board with us. Getting them signed in such an expeditious fashion was one of my best sales efforts.

As I did at Katz, I put in writing for our staff and clients to see what we stood for and what they could expect from us via a vision and mission statement. It was our Sentry "guarantee," a proud proclamation of how we would conduct business—a strategic compass that would serve as a guide for everyone in the company.

The Sentry Mission

We are committed to providing our clients with the best national representation they have ever experienced. Our dealings with our coworkers, clients, and agencies will always be fair, honest, and forthright. Our culture is one of passion, persistence, and performance, and we will always strive to be worthy of our clients' respect, support, trust, and friendship.

The Sentry Vision

We will employ the hardest working, best prepared, most knowledgeable sales staff with the best agency relationships. There will be total commitment from all involved to the creation of a very special company.

Upper management will set a challenging work pace and establish the proper performance expectations. Upper management will always "model" the attitudes, behavior, values, and expectations that we expect our managers, sellers, and assistants to display.

We will strive to ensure that all within the organization feel proud, elevated, and dignified due to their association with this company. Everyone will recognize, understand, and appreciate that they are playing a key role in the building of something special, meaningful, and significant.

Everyone will understand the importance of performance and execution. No matter what the circumstances or obstacles, performance is expected.

This company will be the best place to work. It will never be the easiest, but it will be the best place to learn, grow, and develop. Our culture will be challenging, invigorating, and demanding. Those that work here will deeply believe in and appreciate the importance of relationships, knowledge, and service.

All employees will be challenged to achieve what heretofore was thought to be not possible. Our expectations will be demanding, consistent, and never compromised.

Product mastery as well as relationship mastery will be stressed and coached. We will build and develop the most meaningful agency relationships. Our salespeople will ensure that our client stations' benefits are expertly positioned, appreciated, and understood by the agency community. Our salespeople themselves will also be expertly positioned within the ad community to secure our client's unfair share.

We will enthusiastically respond to the direction, input, and concerns of our clients. This partnership will be the strongest of any current national rep/client relationship. Issues will be discussed honestly and openly and then aggressively addressed. Success for Sentry is client satisfaction.

We understand that customer/client satisfaction is never final. We will continue to look for creative ways to provide our clients and agencies with the most professional and effective sales staff in the business.

Business Lesson #17

Every leader needs a strong #2.

You can be my wingman any time.
—Iceman,
aka Val Kilmer,
Top Gun

My one request to Stu Olds before accepting the Sentry challenge was that I be able to choose my "wingman," in this case, my general sales manager, who possessed the same work ethic and expectations that I did. Peter Burton was an indispensable partner in building out Sentry and was every bit as responsible for its success as I was. He was, and remains, an outstanding radio management and sales executive. Without a strong #2 of similar mind-set, you are whistling in the wind.

Business Lesson #18

Push your limits.

Comfort zones are where dreams go to die.
—Unknown

Never stop. Sentry radio was thriving quite nicely when one year later Olds again asked me to create another company for our largest corporate client, Cap Cities/ABC Radio. The client requested me as president and had I not accepted the position they were likely going to take their business to the competition. So once again, I began the process of creating a new company from scratch. Amcast Radio was born as a dedicated national sales company dedicated to Cap Cities/ABC Radio. As with Sentry, I again had a terrific general sales manager and #2 in Mitch Kline, who again was every bit as responsible for building the company as I was.

Safety is for the retired, and I had another opportunity to reinvent myself with Amcast.

Business Lesson #19

Success is never guaranteed.

The struggle is guaranteed, success is not.

—Unknown

You can't decide how you get knocked down, but you can decide how you pick yourself up. It turns out that this move would be considerably less successful than Sentry. One year later, despite strong performance by our sales team, Cap Cities/ABC fired us and took their business to the competition due to our parent company at the time, Evergreen Media, raiding Cap Cities/ABC's radio network talent. Amcast was now clientless. How does the saying go, "What doesn't kill you makes you stronger?" Stu Olds steadfastly stood by the Amcast team throughout this entire ordeal, but after forty-five days of attempting to sign another client, we had to reassign the salespeople to other KRG companies. As fate would have it, in a few short years, I would be able to pay Stu back for his loyalty as he worked through his most serious professional crisis.

Business Lesson #20

You can go home.

All change is not growth; as all
movement is not forward.

—Ellen Glasgow,
American novelist

You can go home. With the demise of Amcast, I became the executive VP of the KRG, assisting Stu Olds with the oversight of Katz, Christal, Sentry, and Eastman but soon yearned to be on the front lines, leading a team and directly impacting revenue. As fate would have it, Sentry Radio was having some difficulties, so I swapped places with the then president of Sentry and went back to running the company I had built two years earlier. The company was in some cramped quarters, and I noted the size of the president's office, which I thought was overly large in relation to the team's cramped quarters.

My first request was to have my office cut in half to create another office for a senior salesperson who was operating in a cube and who would be thrilled to have an office, even if it were next to mine. I have always believed that the managers/leaders are the "water boys" for their team. In battle, the troops eat first; the generals eat last. In sales, you take care of the salespeople first. It is the way I always tried to manage—via an inverted pyramidal flowchart. The great basketball coach Dean Smith of the University of North Carolina called it "servant leadership." Toro's ex-CEO, Ken Melrose, also referred to leading as "servant leadership" writing in 1995: "Bit by bit I came to realize that you lead best by serving the needs of your people. You don't do their job for them; you enable them to learn and progress on the job."

Business Lesson #21

Sometimes you just need to suck it up.

"Life is all about setbacks. A life lived without disappointment is a life lived in a cocoon. People have recovered from far worse setbacks."

—Tony Clark,
former major leaguer

It was now "character" time. In 2000, the entire Katz Radio Group—consisting of Katz Radio, Christal Radio, Eastman Radio, and Sentry Radio—was sold to Clear Channel Radio, a huge radio broadcaster owner of over one thousand radio stations and an outdoor billboard company. The reason they purchased the Katz Radio Group was they wanted a larger dedicated national sales company to handle national sales for their growing portfolio of radio stations. As a result, Sentry and Eastman salespeople and management merged into Clear Channel's existing national sales arm to form Clear Channel Radio Sales, which had three regional presidents, of which I was one. Another executive became COO of the company, reporting to Olds.

Because of having very successfully overseen Katz Radio and creating two national sales companies from scratch, to say I was disappointed about not getting the COO position would be a gross understatement. It was devastatingly disappointing. The individual who became COO, Mike Agovino, was a dear friend, who replaced me as president of Katz Radio when I created Sentry and one of my early hires in New York and an incredibly talented man. He deserved my loyalty as he had given me his over the years.

I painfully stumbled upon the fact that I had to follow my own belief, which was that to be a good leader you also had to be a good follower. I had no choice but to walk my talk. Professionally, it was the most difficult thing I ever had to do. To make matters, worse on a personal level I was going through a divorce—a challenging time personally and professionally.

Business Lesson #22

Every hand you are dealt can be overcome.

> *It is your reaction to adversity, not*
> *the adversity itself, which determines*
> *how your life's story will develop.*
>
> —Dieter Uchtdorf,
> German aviator

My opportunity to pay back Stu Olds for his support and loyalty during the Amcast dissolution came a few years later, on Friday, November 14, 2003. While he was out of town flying to his mother's eighty-fifth birthday celebration, the presidents of the other Katz Radio Group companies—Katz Radio and Christal Radio—along with all of their employees quit and walked out across the country, going to work for our arch-competitor, Interep—close to two hundred in all.

It was a carefully orchestrated action to coincide with Stu Olds being out of town, which added to the resulting chaos.

The reason it was executed on Friday and when Olds was out of town was because there was a clause in all KRG client agreements that stated it would be a breach of contract if Katz and Christal did not have dedicated offices open and operating to service their clients. This meant Olds not only had to fly back from Wisconsin on the same day but had only forty-eight hours to devise a course of action over the weekend to keep Katz Radio and Christal Radio operational come Monday without any of the Katz and Christal personnel.

The leaders behind this walkout were clearly counting on the fact that come Monday, all Katz and Christal offices would be unmanned, and the KRG would be in breach of contract. Meaning the competitor whom they just joined, Interep, would be able to obtain ownership of these station contracts, worth millions of dollars, at zero cost—a doomsday scenario for Stu Olds.

Olds immediately caught the next flight back to New York, where he; my Clear Channel Radio Sales counterpart, Jeff Howard; Bonnie Press; and I worked all weekend and ended up crippling the "walkout" by transferring fifty-eight Clear Channel Radio Sales and Katz Dimensions managers and salespeople to staff the Katz and Christal offices on Monday morning. There was no breach of contract. The mass defection had failed. The following communication was sent out to all employees:

From: Stu Olds
Sent: Monday, November 17, 2003, 5:16 p.m.
Subject: Letter to all of KMG

Dear Katz Media Group employees,
As you can imagine the last forty-eight hours have been immensely challenging. But once again, we proved we were up to the challenge. The Katz Radio Group is open for business with fifty-eight strong managers and sellers in New York and throughout our regional offices. We are open because Bob McCurdy, Jeff Howard, Bonnie Press, and their staffs raised their hand and asked what they could do to assist in this time of need. We are open because we will not be broken by individuals who want to run our business into the ground by taking our employees and clients with them. We are open because the Katz Media Group established in 1888 has withstood over a century of tumultuous times and continued to succeed and thrive with its reputation of excellence intact.

I want to thank everyone who is stepping outside their regular job description today by taking on additional or unfamiliar responsibilities to handle the Katz and Christal business for our clients and for our company's future. I have received calls and emails of encouragement from the television divisions who offered to pinch-hit to make sure our business is handled properly. I greatly appreciate that support.

Thanks again for making me proud to come to work here every day.

As always, please feel free to contact me with any comments or questions you may have.

Best,
Stu

As a result, there were several hundred ex-Katz and Christal employees at Interep offices across the country with no clients and nothing to do. The next week, after discussions with Olds, they all returned to work at the Katz Media Group. Disaster averted. Masterfully handled by Mr. Olds, who exhibited incredible leadership, grace, and wisdom under extreme circumstances.

It is not an overstatement to say that that weekend changed the course of the national radio representation industry. A few short years later, Interep went out of business.

Business Lesson #23

Never allow yourself to grow old in your job.

*Keep on pushing the boundaries and
reaching for higher heights.*

—Puff Daddy,
American rapper

Why stop now? In 2009, Stu Olds again asked me to accept another career challenge by overseeing the KRG's new business development efforts for the radio industry, which needed a jolt. At first I hesitated, as this job was completely different from any position I previously held.

In the end, I ultimately believed I could make a difference, and the idea of dealing with advertisers at the chief marketing officer level and the CEO level at the agencies was appealing. Despite being fifty-eight, I was too young to coast. Taking that position was a terrific decision. I learned more about advertising and marketing in the next four years than I had the previous fifteen. Clear Channel, now iHeartRadio, and other broadcasters are now pursuing many of the suggestions I had recommended a decade earlier. As with Katz, Sentry, and Amcast, I was extremely fortunate to have a dynamic #2 in Greg Glenday, who was so key to our success.

Business Lesson #24

Above all, be true to yourself.

Happiness is when what you think, what you say, and what you do are in harmony.
—Mahatma Gandhi,
political ethicist

Do what you know is right for you. Eighteen months later, Stu Olds unexpectedly passed away, which was a terrible blow to the company and devastating to me personally. He had been a close friend and partner for almost three decades.

Shortly after Olds's passing, our parent company, Clear Channel, wanted me to leave Katz (the Katz Radio Group was owned by Clear Channel) and oversee their research/marketing division, which I initially resisted. After multiple discussions and some arm-twisting, I accepted the position, but it did not feel right. I later notified Clear Channel that I had changed my mind—that I was a "sales" guy and not a researcher—and decided to stay to oversee new business development at the Katz Radio Group. It was an extremely difficult decision and one that did not endear me to our parent company's hierarchy, but it was the right decision for me.

As Hamlet said, "This above all; to thine own self be true."

Business Lesson #25

Trust your Gut; follow your heart.

Trust your instincts. Intuition doesn't lie.
—Oprah Winfrey,
American television personality

All things must pass. Over the next several years, the structure of our new business effort was in flux, and my zeal for the position was already waning when a new CEO came on board to oversee the Katz Radio Group. I gave it about six weeks but ultimately decided that I could not work with or for this individual. So again, above all, always be true to yourself no matter how painful it might be.

After four years of being president of the Katz Marketing Solutions division and after being president of four of the corporation's companies—Katz, Sentry, and Amcast, and co-president of Clear Channel Radio Sales—I decided it was time to leave. Unquestionably, it was unnerving walking away from a company after thirty-four years, but I knew it was time. I had confidence in my abilities to handle whatever would come next.

Business Lesson #26

Good things happen to those who work hard.

Suddenly you just know it is time to start something
new and trust the magic of new beginnings.

—Unknown

When I left Katz, I said that I would no longer work with anyone I did not want to work with. What came next was a call from Heather Monahan, the Beasley Media Group's CRO, one of the few radio companies I had not worked with over the past three decades, and asked if I'd assist her with a couple of Beasley markets.

Soon thereafter, I was consulting Beasley, also picking up another client, Alpha Media. I was consulting from the basement of an office building in Westport, Connecticut, with one tiny window and a squirrel that visited several times a day for peanuts. I loved it. The best part was that the executives at Beasley and Alpha were outstanding individuals.

I had no assistants to help me—no help desk to call regarding computer issues—and it was great. Several years later the Beasley Media Group, led by Caroline Beasley, Bruce Beasley, and Brian Beasley asked me to join them full time, which I did, because I felt they were terrific people and exceptional media professionals. It was an extremely gratifying decision, and I think the world of each of them.

CHAPTER 5

Leadership

A leader is one who knows the way,
goes the way and shows the way.

—John C. Maxwell,
American author

Each of these life and business lessons contributed to me becoming the leader I became. Leaders and the art of leadership always fascinated me. At a young age, I soon realized a coach in sports makes a huge difference in terms of teaching and motivation. Upon entering the workforce, I quickly saw the same thing. A good leader is a company's "X" factor.

Way back in the late 1970s when I first got into management in Indianapolis, someone asked me how I would define success. I thought about it for a while and replied simply that it would be the number of people who upon retirement would say that I was someone they worked for that made a difference in their careers and lives. I have never been able to improve upon that definition. Money has never been my motivation. I have always found it is better to be guided by a strong ideology, ironclad values, and a sense of purpose beyond the pursuit of the buck.

I always admired UCLA's basketball coach, John Wooden, not only for the way he led but the way in which he lived his life. I will never forget him interviewed immediately after UCLA had just lost in the NCAA semifinals to North Carolina State in 1974 and how composed and gracious he was in defeat after such a disappointing loss. Duke's Coach K, Dean Smith, and the other great ones behaved similarly. I thought to myself, that is leadership! Unbeknownst to me at the time, Coach Wooden ended up having more impact on my leadership philosophy than anyone with the possible exception of Stu Olds.

My senior year in college was Coach Wooden's last year at UCLA in 1975, and I reached out to him for some career advice. Prior to getting into coaching full time, he had been an English teacher and high school coach, and I was looking to do the same.

Fast-forward fifteen years to 1990. I was going to be on the West Coast, and I contacted him to see if he would be available for lunch. We got together, and for the next twenty years until his passing in 2010, I ventured out to his condominium in Encino three or four times a year and communicated often via phone and mail. My second wife, Sydney, used to call him Johnny, which he loved. Sydney and our combined seven kids went out to visit Coach on a number of occasions. He was also gracious enough to allow me to invite my clients to many of our lunches. To this day, I still hear from ex-clients how thankful they are for having the opportunity to spend some time with Coach Wooden.

When you were with Coach Wooden in his small den for an afternoon, it was a time to be treasured. I used to marvel that despite him being in his late nineties, he was still making appointments months down the road.

When you were in the presence of Coach Wooden, you were in the presence of an individual who perfected the art of living as closely as anyone ever has. Two of his favorite people were Abraham Lincoln and Mother Teresa. Two perfect role models, and he did love his poetry. At ninety-nine, his mind was incredibly sharp as he recited poem after poem.

Mitch Kupchak, then the general manager of the Los Angeles Lakers and currently the general manager of the Charlotte Hornets, often accompanied me to see Coach and we were like two kids sitting in the presence of a grand master. As Mitch and I were leaving Coach's condominium one afternoon after I told Coach I had to go and catch a plane, I recall Mitch saying to me, "You just can't get up and tell Coach it is time to leave. He should tell you when it's time." I replied, "Mitch, it is Friday afternoon, and if I don't get home for the weekend, my wife is going to kill me. In this case, Sydney trumps Coach Wooden."

Contrary to what some might think, people are not born leaders. Good leadership is an acquired "skill" that can be refined just as any skill can be refined.

The nice thing about refining leadership skills is that you need not do it alone. Hundreds of terrific books, articles, and podcasts deal with this topic. I recall Coach Wooden saying to me one time that "reading is listening." At first, it didn't click, but then it sunk in—when you read, you are in essence "listening" to the words and thoughts of the greatest leaders, scholars, teachers who ever lived. What could be better?

Leadership lessons are often on display, live on the TV during news conferences, political debates, the Sunday morning talk shows, or any sporting event. When watching a game, I often spend as much time watching the coach on the sidelines as the event itself. I want to see how coaches handle themselves in stressful situations, how their team relates to them during timeouts, how they relate to assistant coaches, how their assistant coaches relate to them, how the players interact with them when coming off the field or court. It is a real-time study in leadership with so many valuable lessons to observe.

Throughout my career, I always stressed the importance of knowledge, but just being knowledgeable does not always translate to being a good leader. Engineers are knowledgeable but that does not make them great leaders. Great leaders need more than expertise. The average leader usually possesses expertise. The good leader possesses expertise and can effectively communicate it, but the great leader possesses expertise, can effectively communicate it, and can inspire. The ability to inspire separates the great from the good leader. Great leaders should also be good storytellers, but stories need to be based on reality and not fairy tales.

The exceptional leader is consistently able to get the individuals on his or her team to narrow the gap between what they are currently accomplishing versus what they are capable of accomplishing. He or she gets the people to push the boundaries of their own potential, which is not easy. Effective leaders are consistently able to get their teams to accept short-term pain for long-term gain in the pursuit of a common goal. This is a special and acquired skill.

There was always an unspoken rule at any company or team I led, which was, anyone, regardless of title, could do what I could do. There were never different sets of rules for those in management and those in sales. Nor should there be. Additionally, I would never expect them to do anything I would not be willing to do. They knew this. The best leadership is always leadership by example.

Another rule I tried to live by was that if someone "felt" something, they could voice it, as feelings are real and should not go unstated if they were communicated professionally. Paying attention to employee feelings matters. I might not have liked or agreed with what was always stated but everyone had the right to express themselves. I am sure some would confirm that I was not always perfect here, and they are correct, but I did try.

Effective leadership is challenging. Everything a leader does, says, does not do, or does not say is being noted by the staff. As such, an effective leader must have an absolute sense of true north when making decisions. What is right is simply right regardless of the circumstances or who is involved. Expediency should never usurp doing the right thing. People respect this. There is a simplicity and purity to this type of decision-making. To get to this point, effective leaders need to inoculate themselves from the overwhelming human desire to be "liked" when making decisions. Effective leaders do not make different decisions for different people. They are consistent. Their teams know what they can expect. This even-keeled consistency contributes to their ability to lead effectively. What is right is always right, and successful leaders always figure out a way to do what is right and not expedient.

Someone asked me if there is formula for leadership success. I replied that I could not give them an exact formula for success, but I could give them a formula for failure, and that would be trying to please everyone. Trying to please everyone ultimately ends up pleasing no one. Leadership is not a popularity contest. What is right is not always popular, and what is popular is not always right, but doing what's "right" wins long term.

CHAPTER 6

Corporate Culture

Culture eats strategy for breakfast.
—Peter Drucker,
American management consultant

I always felt that my most important job as a leader was to create the right culture, and if I got that right, everything else would fall into place. I spent a tremendous amount of time trying to accomplish this. Culture comes about based on what you do, not what you say. The most important thing that separates one company from another is its culture, and companies with the strongest corporate cultures can pass them down from generation to generation.

A strong culture can help a company weather any crisis. Without one, you are lost. An effective culture leads to alignment, and there is a direct correlation between alignment and strong business performance.

Culture is what takes over when management is not around and during those stressful moments of truth when key decisions are required. It is what a company's employees do daily and how they behave. It is an organization's true north.

Building a strong corporate culture requires focus and an unwavering commitment to reinforcing its guiding principles.

There can be no "days off" when building the right culture, as culture happens either by design or by default. As leaders, either you direct the culture or the culture directs you, and if it directs you, it more often embraces expediency. The only thing that evolves by itself in an organization is underperformance.

There is nothing deeply mysterious about a corporate culture; it is simply the level of foundational assumptions and beliefs shared by members of an organization. These values, beliefs, and assumptions comprise the bedrock of the organization and need to be constantly reinforced. Getting those foundational assumptions and beliefs shared by all is the leader's biggest challenge.

The shaping of a corporate culture is more than half done when hiring, which makes it critical to bring on board people who share the same values. They need not execute their responsibilities exactly the same, but the top-line, bone-deep values need to be similar. I have always attempted to build cultures that are good, fair, and tough. Good and fair to each other but tough on expectations and performance.

A company's culture is the essence of its soul—the norms and expectations of its employees, their approach and commitment to their jobs. What is acceptable but, more importantly, what is unacceptable. It should be a culture that embraces change but despite "change," its cultural principles remain rock solid.

A strong culture brings a stability, focus, and direction to a company in the face of an ever-changing and chaotic business environment. We always attempted to codify it to ensure a consistent level of personnel quality and performance across the company and found that it positively boosted performance, talent attraction, and retention.

One way we perpetuated our culture was that we made it hard as hell to be hired, under the premise of what is hardest earned is most valued and appreciated. We had many different selling styles throughout the company but when it came to work ethic and the expectation of excellence, it was one company indivisible.

Assessing "fit" is difficult. It was not unusual to have candidates come back a half dozen times or more before extending an offer, as the price of hiring the wrong individual was extremely steep in terms of lost training time and future revenue. All levels within the organization were involved with the hiring process—corporate, sales management, and salespeople—as hiring the right talent was too important of a job to rely on the judgement of one individual.

We made sure that all new hires were familiar with the company's history, tradition, and philosophy, understanding the responsibility they had in perpetuating the company's level of excellence. They soon realized that they were becoming part of something much bigger than each of them individually—a company with a set of rules that is on a mission with an imaginary sign above the front entrance stating, "Only the best of the best can work here." We wanted them to think of their jobs and the company as something special, with a heritage to be preserved and built-upon.

One key part of the acculturation process was our training program, which I referenced earlier. Training and acculturation was too important of a responsibility to turn it over to anyone but our sales management team. Our managers invested their sweat and time outside their normal responsibilities to train these new hires, which resulted in a strong bond with the newly hired and provided us with the morale authority to challenge them to stretch in search of their potential. Our training programs were intense, requiring total commitment, communicating that the only entitlement moving forward is contributing to the company and that it is not an entitlement to be here. Perform or be gone.

The program embraced the phrase *Tabula rasa*, or "Everyone starts from zero." We wanted all within the program to forget what they thought they knew about sales and open their minds to what they were about to learn. We then built them up into smarter, harder-working, more effective versions of their previous selves.

Via our actions, one of the takeaways training program graduates walked away with (many washed out of the program—a broken engagement is preferable to a broken marriage) was that we did not expect anything of them we did not expect of ourselves.

Another key benefit of management's involvement in the program was that it instilled a tremendous amount of loyalty toward the company. These trainees knew how much we cared about them after six weeks in the program and the amount of personal time and money we invested in them to succeed. There are few things more motivating to employees than seeing their managers invest their sweat to assist them in growing professionally. Often a lifelong bond resulted.

The Katz training program was unique to the radio industry in the 1980s and served the company well for several decades, teaching the newly hired their first leadership lesson, which is self-mastery. Peak performers needed to be buttoned-up, know their material cold, and able to present it flawlessly. The training program was unquestionably extreme. It had to be, as we were hiring individuals with little to no sales experience who upon graduation had to outperform experienced competition.

From the first minute of the program, we worked hard to get the new hires to take on the values of the company as their own, as we understood that some of these rookies would someday be the future leaders of the company. The program also created a culture that reinforced and encouraged people to contribute as much as they can, not as little as they can, which lead to empowerment and not micromanagement.

Over time, due to our success, many of our key senior managers were transferred to sister companies—Christal Radio and Eastman Radio—to shore them up with strong executive talent. This resulted in more competition for us as we were now directly competing against executives we had trained. This just served to push us harder and raise our game. The competitive side of me was not thrilled with this, but as a leader you always want to see your people develop, expand their responsibilities, and grow your leadership tree.

The training program was only one part of the acculturation process. The norms and expectations of the Katz salesperson and sales manager set the tone for the culture, as did the three booklets that I wrote, as did my frequent communication with the salespeople and sales managers.

CHAPTER 7

Putting It All into Practice

No company, small or large, can win over the long
run without energized employees who believe in
a mission and understand how to achieve it.

—Jack Welch,
former CEO General Electric

My communication to the management and sales staff played a key role in the continued acculturation of the company.

What follows are "radiograms" (Katz internal email before email) as well as emails that I have forwarded to Katz sales managers, salespeople, rising stars, and trainees from 1987 to 1995. The goal of this communication was to further acculturate and ensure that everyone in the company understood what was expected and that we were all rowing in the same direction.

These grams and emails enabled me to "touch" every sales manager and salesperson several times per week, maintaining my visibility with them across the country. More importantly, they served to reinforce the company's expectations. It also provided me with an opportunity to interact with staff one-on-one, responding to their replies to what I had written. Some were light, some were motivational, and some minced few words. One thing I always made clear is that I was there to assist any way possible. I always tried to be consistent in my messaging. You will notice many of the same foundational themes from my life and business lessons in many of these missives:

➢ Hard Work
➢ Integrity
➢ Knowledge
➢ Preparation
➢ Responsibility
➢ Discipline
➢ Performance
➢ Attitude
➢ Effort
➢ Teamwork

I have also included some "Sunday" emails I forwarded to the Beasley sales management team from 2017 to 2020. I was able to locate bits and pieces of written communication from the Sentry, Amcast, and Clear Channel years but obviously did a better job of retaining the Katz and more recent Beasley communication than the others. Much of the Sentry, Amcast, and Clear Channel communication focused on similar topics as the Katz and Beasley material. I tried to keep these radiograms and emails short and focused on a specific theme, never passing up an opportunity to teach and coach. Read on and you will see first-hand how a culture of performance was built and maintained. What is old is new, and what is new is old. Everything below is as applicable today as ever.

The following material appears as originally sent.

My General Sales Manager Katz Years

To: All Katz Sellers and Managers
From: Bob McCurdy
Re: Marriage
4/17/87 11:44 a.m.

I read something the other day that really caught my eye. It was in one of the business magazines, and they quoted the executive as follows: "The sale merely consummates the courtship, then the marriage begins. How good the marriage is depends upon how well the relationship is "managed" by the seller, not the client." The natural tendency in relationships, whether it be marriage or business, is atrophy—the erosion or deterioration of sensitivity and attentiveness. A healthy relationship in marriage or in business requires a constant and conscious fight against the forces of atrophy. The same article went on to quote that it costs seven to eight times as much to go out and secure a new client than to keep the one you currently have.

We recently picked up a number of new clients. Now the marriage begins. We need to show them exactly what it means to be a Katz client. There is never a second opportunity for a first impression.

We have represented many of our clients for a number of years—in some cases, decades—and the tendency might be to take them for granted. We can't allow this to happen. Let's make the extra effort with our existing clients to make sure they understand just how important they are to us and how proud we are to be working with them as well.

Thanks, and have a super Easter weekend.

To: All Katz Managers
From: Bob McCurdy
Re: Sales prospects
1/26/88 1:25 p.m.

Everyone is familiar with our training program, which thus far has produced a number of solid salespeople. Let's keep in mind that the training program doesn't do away with the need for identifying strong sales talent in your market. Do not expect if an opening occurs in your office that you will automatically be assigned a training program graduate.

Stay close with your "prospects" in your market selling yourself and the company. The bottom line is that we will continue to support you through the training program when possible, but the ultimate responsibility for identifying and hiring top-notch sales talent is yours. This should become part of your daily routine.

To: Jeff Weinand
From: Bob McCurdy
Re: Your promotion
2/22/88 2:44 p.m.

Jeff,
You are being transferred to the Motor City as an account executive, and we're counting on you to be absolutely the best. Remember to keep the following in mind that we discussed:

Service the hell out of your agencies and clients. You are no longer a rookie but an experienced salesperson who is being transferred to Detroit to stabilize the office. You will be dealing with clients with whom you had very little contact in New York. Make them Weinand fans.

Continue to expand your knowledge base not only of our

markets but also of the buyers and agencies. Penetrate your agencies vertically and horizontally so that you are known by all.

Know your regional markets better than anyone. They are your bread and butter. Live those markets. These clients are used to excellence. I know you will take that definition up several notches.

Jeff, Detroit has had some outstanding Katz sellers over the years and has a legacy of dominance. I believe you will not only maintain that legacy but build upon it. Best of luck. See you soon and thanks for being the best.

Remember that first impressions are lasting impressions!

To: All Katz Managers
From: Bob McCurdy
Re: Sellers
2/23/88 3:14 p.m.

If I am to believe that our competitors only have below average reps, then I have got to wonder why we're not doing a 30 share of revenue. If they are as inept as I'm told, why is it so difficult for us to increase our revenue share? A couple of things. First, the competition is not as bad as I am hearing, and second, you have to pan a lot of sand to find gold. Same with identifying strong sales talent. Let's start "panning" for salespeople more consistently.

To: All Katz Managers and Sellers
From: Bob McCurdy
Re: Sloppy
1/21/88 1:51 p.m.

Over the past week, I have received three phone calls from clients expressing concern about how hard we are selling their stations. We all know what our clients expect of us is not unreasonable. Let's not get sloppy and happy. Do the fundamentals and communicate your efforts to every one of our clients. While we can't close every sale, we can make our clients feel comfortable that we are fighting like hell on their behalf.

If for some reason you can't do this, tell your manager, and he will reassign the agency. If you don't want to do it, let us know and we will find someone who will. It is SOP that we explore every sales angle to get our clients sold every time. These types of phone call stop today, right?

To: All Katz Managers
From: Bob McCurdy
Re: Vacations
4/5/88 10:54 a.m.

We have never been overly stringent with vacations. When you need one, you take it. We have never policed the number of vacation days managers take. If you tell us you need one, go.

We have a business to run, and I have got to know who is and isn't in the office. If you are out of the office for whatever reason, let me know. Let's tighten this up and at least give the appearance we know what we're doing.

To: All Katz Manager and Sellers
From: Bob McCurdy
Re: Los Angeles
4/6/88 4:00 p.m.

Effective immediately I will be everyone's contact for all Los Angeles business opportunities. Additionally, I remain the point contact for all Miami and Detroit business. So, when you think of Los Angeles, Miami, or Detroit think of McCurdy. Call me first with a strategy that you will utilize to maximize revenue for these three markets before you call our clients. I will attempt to enhance it.

Thanks in advance for being superb when selling these markets.

To: All Katz Managers
From: Bob McCurdy
Re: Rumors
7/18/88 1:15 p.m.

Yesterday a seller asked me about the truth to rumors he'd been hearing for the previous two weeks. He said he had heard it from no less than eleven individuals regarding the validity of the rumor. The depth and detail he went into describing what he thought was about to happen was both absurd and laughable. This salesperson readily admitted that his performance had suffered due to these rumors. Over the past several years, there has been other similar examples.

When we discuss sensitive topics with you, we need to know it will remain confidential. I think we are becoming grand masters at the "telephone" game that we used to play as kids.

If you have any questions regarding company direction, just ask. Is reality a whole lot less juicy than the rumor? Yep. When you get right down to it, an important trait necessary for career advancement is the ability to keep confidential information confidential. Got it?

To: All Katz Managers and Sellers
From: Bob McCurdy
Re: Misc.
9/12/88 1:58 p.m.

In real estate, the most important factor is location, location, location. In sales, it is basics, basics, basics. What a beautiful and simple business.

Good selling!

To: All Katz Managers and Sellers
From: Bob McCurdy
Re: Houston & Sacramento
11/3/88 1:48 p.m.

Since becoming the point person in Houston, I have been involved with three pieces of business, one of which was a one-day flight. In Sacramento, I have been involved with five pieces of business.

I will be blunt and to the point. There is no way across the entire country that there are only three pieces of business in Houston and five pieces of business in Sacramento pending. I am the point person for these markets for a reason—to be involved with helping you close the order. If I am not contacted, I can't be involved, and if I am not involved, I can't help close the order and get some needed billing for these important clients. Let's get these markets fixed—together.

To: All Katz Managers
From: Bob McCurdy
Re: Sports Sales
11/9/88 1:44 p.m.

Let me start off by saying I appreciated everyone's candor on the conference call. I think, though, that some of us approached it as though we had a choice whether we sold sports or not. We do not.

Not only do sports sales generate big billing, but also they are 100 percent share dollars that contribute to our overall company and market share, particularly in sensitive markets.

Our lives both personally and professionally are one big "priority" list. Personally, you make decisions that provide the most gratification. Professionally, we don't always have complete control of what becomes a priority. There is no choice here, guys; we need to perform.

As a manager, what's important to you becomes important to your team. It is that simple. You are the conscience of your office. And what's important to your salespeople needs to be upping their sports sales game. Let's get out there and sell Dodgers, Tigers, and Royals, now!

To: All Katz Managers
From: Bob McCurdy
Re: Sports
12/12/88 10:13 a.m.

Evidently, my eloquent pleas to up our game selling sports has fallen on deaf ears. One client recently referred to our spots sales efforts as "indifferent," and I sure as hell agree. On 12/1, a radiogram went out requesting an update on the thirty-plus target accounts we discussed. Only four offices responded. This type of response is acceptable at Katz? Never was and never will be.

I will repeat it again; we have no higher priority than to get these sports packages sold.

Any managers or sellers who feel as if they can't make the commitment to get this done, have them submit their resignation to me, and we will get someone in there who will get it done.

One of the responsibilities of a manager is to anticipate and prevent crises. If we don't change direction fast here, we will be right in the middle of a huge one. We are all better than this!

To: Mike Agovino/Steve Moskowitz
From: Bob McCurdy
Re: Neatness
12/1/88 4:03 p.m.

No, I haven't been transformed into Felix Unger, but I will tell you guys I am getting tired of walking around the office and seeing paper littering the floor near the Xerox machine. I can't tell you how many times I have reached down to pick up the paper off the floor trying to set an example. I am now officially tired of being the only one doing this, and it seems as if I am the only one who picks up towels off the men's bathroom floor as well. Also for the record, I am tired of picking up paper clips and rubber bands off the floor as people walk by. This morning I purposely did not pick up a piece of paper outside the men's room, and it was still there a few minutes ago. I don't want to be an asshole, but let's get this in gear. We don't have to be spit and polish, but I think we all expect a neater office environment. I hope you will address this in your weekly meeting and cover with the assistants.

CHAPTER 8

My Katz President Years

To: All Katz Managers and Sellers
From: Bob McCurdy
Re: Reading, Pa.
2/16/93 4:07 p.m.

Mike Shannon is my "professional" brother. Mike Shannon due to him being a client is part of the Katz family. Mike Shannon is a friend, and his billing is pacing appreciably behind last year's. Mike Shannon put his ass on the line by coming to Katz in spite of a record year by his former rep. Mike Shannon bought into us and what we stand for and how we approach our jobs. It took me two years to convince Mike Shannon that he'd be better off at Katz. We cannot accept anything but excellent performance in Reading. To those managers who have yet to have a conversation with Mike, may I suggest the time has come? Get involved. Be proactive. Nothing less will be accepted. Think of Shannon's WRFY FM as a Katz O&O. It is time to unleash every ounce of sales acumen and sales tool in our arsenal to increase WRFY revenue.

To: All Katz Managers and Sellers
From: Bob McCurdy
Re: RASP
2/18/93 2:35 p.m.

We have a very important challenge facing us. I do believe it is larger than any of us believe. It is about "process." The process of arming ourselves with the best sales ammunition possible. The thing that is startling and concerning here is that each of us, by not doing our small part in keeping this system current, are hurting only ourselves and our ability to generate revenue.

What do I know? Apparently, everyone thinks not a lot when it comes to this subject. The only thing I do know is that we are not as good as we can be without an up-to-date RASP system. We need to get this in gear. Please get us your thoughts. We are better than this.

To: All Katz Manager and Sellers
From: Bob McCurdy
Re: Why
3/31/93 9:27 a.m.

Everybody has seen the Budweiser commercial that asks, "Why ask why?," well I am going to ask "Why?"

"Why" is it that some sellers and managers can stay within their expense budgets?

"Why" is it that some offices can get their expenses in on time?

Now I'm going to ask "What?" What are you going to do about it?

To: All Katz Managers
From: Bob McCurdy
Re: Solicitation
4/2/93 4:17 p.m.

As you know, there are few things as effective as a great letter of endorsement from an existing client. As you also might know, from time to time we solicit new clients.

You also might be interested to know that the initial response to my email requesting additional letters of existing client endorsements was lower than the response to direct mail touting discounts on root canals.

Every time you talk to a client or we do something spectacularly good, ask them for a note expressing their satisfaction with Katz.

It's a great support to our solicitation effort … thanks and while this gram is atypically "light," this is a serious request.

To: All Managers and Sellers
From: Bob McCurdy
Re: Seeds
4/8/92 5:50 p.m.

We all know how tiny seeds grow into trees. Even Kareem Abdul Jabbar and Hulk Hogan were small at one time, just as there was a time when Michael Jordan couldn't dunk, and Madonna couldn't sing.

So, what's the point? The point is as sure as you are reading this, there are stations on our list that are in their growth stage or have recently changed formats. Take it to the bank some of these stations will become big revenue producers for us as they develop. As such, it is expected that we sell and position these properties with the same zest and zeal as we sell our top-ranked stations.

We will make our current and future lives simpler, more fun, and prosperous by doing so.

To: All Katz Managers and Sellers
From: Bob McCurdy
Re: Impermanent
4/28/93 6:51 a.m.

Read an article the other day that hit home. There was a line in the article that said, "Success at best is an impermanent achievement, which can always slip out of hand." We've all been doing a great job, but the past doesn't amount to a hill of beans. In fact, past successes have a habit of contributing to the downfall of successful companies. Each day we need to go out there and re-prove ourselves to our clients and buyers, looking for ways to improve ourselves. If we continue to focus and execute, we'll be in good shape. Now is not the time to get complacent. Now is the time to turn up the heat—on the competition. If we keep caring and performing, we will ensure to maintain the growth each of us has been so instrumental in creating. Thanks!

To: All Katz Managers and Sellers
From: Bob McCurdy
Re: Eating
4/29/93 6:37 a.m.

What do eating and learning have in common? You never graduate from eating; you have got to do it to survive and thrive. The same is true with learning. Set aside fifteen minutes/day to learn something new or to refine a skill. At home, I tell my kids, you gotta eat, you gotta take a bath, and you gotta keep learning.

This discipline enables us to separate ourselves from the competition. Let's maintain this competitive edge. Keep learning.

To: All Katz Managers and Sellers
From: Bob McCurdy
Re: Preparation
5/3/93 7:48 a.m.

Mark Twain said, "It takes two weeks to prepare for an impromptu speech." Bobby Knight said, "Everyone wants to succeed, but few people are willing to prepare to succeed." Someone else said, "The will to succeed is important, but what's more important is the will to prepare."

It's funny how everything appears effortless when you are prepared. Preparation breeds confidence, which contributes to sales. Katz, the best. We have no equal, and it's no accident—one major reason is preparation.

To: All Katz Managers and Sellers
From: Bob McCurdy
Re: Luck
5/4/93 9:40 a.m.

We make our own. You've heard it before … "Luck when preparation meets opportunity." Have always figured that luck had a peculiar attachment to work. Work and preparation always keep popping up in the same sentences as luck. It's a jungle out there, and we are our clients' machetes because we work hard at being lucky. Not one of my best analogies, but it's the best I could do this morning. Put your machete to good use today in the media jungle.

Good luck!

To: All Katz Managers and Sellers
From: Bob McCurdy
Re: Change (Growth)
5/24/93 8:15 a.m.

Change is one of the most feared words in the English language. Last week in management meetings, we were discussing how skill wise the national radio salesperson skills have changed very little over the past thirty years. We rep a lot more stations, have developed better systems and support, but our selling skills have changed very little. Would we feel comfortable going to a dentist or doctor who is operating the way they did in 1965?

We'd be interested in your honest feedback/comments regarding the challenges facing us ... how do we alter our sales approach to meet the challenges of the '90s. Please give this the thought it deserves; nothing need be in writing. Call if you'd like, but give us the benefit of your insights as to what we as a company and sales staff need to continue to do to improve ... you know Mike's and my number ...

Thanks, and have a great weekend after we finish Friday with a bang.

To: All Katz Managers and Sellers
From: Bob McCurdy
Re: Brevity
5/17/93 11:51 a.m.

Volume doesn't sell. A clear, concise, hard-hitting presentation does. A one-page document that is well written is more effective than eight pages loosely tied together ... just like a well-written radiogram. There is genius in brevity. Goodbye.

To: Peter Kleiner
From: Bob McCurdy
Re: Car 54, where are you?
5/18/93 8:59 a.m.

I could say the same thing about our Philadelphia suburban sales effort lately. We've been embarrassed once; let's not go for two. Get Muldoon in the office next to yours to assist ... but please do something.

To: All Katz Managers and Sellers
From: Bob McCurdy
Re: Experiencing it
5/21/93 7:18 a.m.

Henry Ford once said, "You don't learn to drive by watching." Same goes for selling, penetrating agencies, handling an unwired avail, doing lunch and learns. Ultimately, if we are to grow, we've got to take the plunge. The courage to take ourselves out of our comfort zone. Putting yourself in a position where you might fail and even be slightly embarrassed is what makes people successful. It's like being at the beach when it is hot. The water is cold, but taking a plunge is better than going in gradually. Each of us knows where we need to take the plunge. Commit to doing it, and you will not only be a more accomplished professional, but the company will be stronger as well.

To: All Katz Managers and Sellers
From: Bob McCurdy
Re: Guests
6/4/93 8:20 a.m.

Came across a comment the other day that is on target. This one guy was describing customer service and how they treated clients the same way they treat house guests. Got me thinking ... we have a ton of visiting clients. When we have houseguests, we go out of our way to ensure that they are comfortable. In fact, it could be argued that our visiting professional "guests" are more important than regular houseguests because without visiting clients, we probably wouldn't even have houses.

Have a great weekend. How can we elevate our visiting client's experiences?

To: All Katz Managers and Sellers
From: Bob McCurdy
Re: Inches
6/11/93 2:58 p.m.

It's the little things that make a difference. The fundamentals. Doing one hundred things 1 percent better. The year that Jack Nicklaus won $228,000 in prize money, he averaged a 70.3 per round. Bob Charles, a good golfer in his own right, averaged a 70.9. Yet Bob only won $48,000. There is an inch of difference between the great and very good golfer. Same in sales.

Have a great weekend.

To: All Katz Managers and Sellers
From: Bob McCurdy
Re: Banking
6/22/93 7:14 a.m.

Think of your relationships with clients and your buyers like your bank account with withdrawals and deposits. There are many different ways we can build up deposits with clients or buyers—prompt service, strong communication, going above and beyond, etc. When business is not pending, look for ways to generate more value for our clients in the buyer's eyes. By doing this, we are increasing our deposits for when we might need a withdrawal down the road. As with our personal bank accounts, your professional accounts must have more deposits than withdrawals so that when you need a favor, you have enough in the bank to cover it.

To: All Katz Managers and Sellers
From: Bob McCurdy
Re: Mary Kay
7/13/93 7:49 a.m.

Was eating breakfast over the weekend, and it was quiet for a change. All four kids were at a basketball camp. My wife had received something in the mail from Mary Kay, and it seemed more interesting than the cereal box. There was a quote, "No matter how busy you are, you must take time to make the other person feel important."

We are all rushed, and sometimes it comes across that way. If we keep the above in mind it might take us another fifteen to thirty seconds to finish the conversation or phone call, but if we did make the extra effort to make the other person feel important, I'd bet it would be the best time we could spend and come back to us in spades. There's no doubt we all keep crazy schedules, but if we keep this quote in mind, we would probably do better business.

To: All Katz Managers and Sellers
From: Bob McCurdy
Re: Vacation
7/27/93 1:42 p.m.

I am outa here this afternoon for vacation and will be back 8/9. Do one thing for me when I am gone. Just one little itsy, bitsy thing … sell the hell out of KABC.

　Thanks!

To: All Katz Managers and Sellers
From: Bob McCurdy
Re: Grand Rapids
8/25/93 8:05 a.m.

The timing of my memo yesterday was uncanny. Today we just dodged a bullet in Grand Rapids. We were getting fired, and McGavren was going to pick up representation. If it wasn't for Tim's and Mike's quick response and the relationship we had with this client, these guys were history.

　Continued success in business is not a destination but a constant process. Unlike sports, there is no clock in business, so winning is never final. The bell never goes off; we have just got to continue selling and winning.

　This company has been built upon hard work. We focus on the fundamentals, which lead to more sales, and our focus on the fundamentals has led to our dominance—for now.

　It is time to get pissed off. Interep has put a full-court press attempting to solicit our clients. You keep protecting what we got, and I will keep taking what they got via our solicitation efforts. Deal?

To: All Katz Managers and Sellers
From: Bob McCurdy
Re: Managers Meeting
9/28/93 5:04 p.m.

The theme for this year's meeting will be Katz The Best-Ever. We've had some terrific managers and sellers pass through these Katz doors over the years. How do we stack up against them?

Our mission as we move into 1994 has got to be more than just being the best out there today. Let's compare ourselves to history. With a focused, determined effort, we can accomplish this and prove to all that we have the best management and sales staff ever assembled under one rep company's roof. To accomplish this, we need to compete against our own potential. Pat Riley talks about "career best efforts" … sounds like a good challenge for us as well.

Seller for seller, manager for manager, assistant for assistant, our challenge is to be the best ever. This is absolutely doable if we make the necessary commitment, manage with courage, and do our jobs the way we know how … a little audacity is good for the soul.

See you guys soon. Remember CBE.

To: All Katz Managers and Sellers
From: Bob McCurdy
Re: Barnstable
10/7/93 2:40 p.m.

No pussyfooting around. We are not getting the job done for Harrisburg and Memphis. In Harrisburg, the station could be doing the billing we're doing if they didn't even have a national rep. It's hand-to-hand combat in Harrisburg, and we're getting our butts kicked left and right.

Memphis. I have to figure out a way to put this mildly—we have rolled over and played dead. We're pacing 50 percent for September with October looking just as bad. Ugly, unacceptable, and worst of all, embarrassing.

These stations need to be aggressively sold and positioned, not just submitted. Our performance in these two markets is quite disturbing.

Everyone look deep inside, dig deep inside, and get these fine stations their unfair share that they deserve. That is what Katz is about, right?

If you need anything, call me, Agovino, Kleiner, or O'Malley. Attention, focus, and discipline will get this fixed.

Let's go. Make it personal.

To: All Katz Managers and Sellers
From: Bob McCurdy
Re: Reflection
11/9/93 7:39 a.m.

We move fast, and we're all tired at the end of the day. We all want to go home, go out, or whatever, but how many of us take a few minutes to reflect upon the day, reflect upon what we've learned, what we could do differently, how we can improve?

Whenever I've been hit with the youthfulness of this company, I respond that experience without learning means nothing. A ten-year vet could be repeating his first year in the business 10x.

The only way we get to improve is by incorporating some reflection in our day. Experiences aren't truly ours until we analyze them, think about them, examine them, question them, and finally understand them.

Do this, and we can be our own best teachers.

To: All Katz Managers and Sellers
From: Bob McCurdy
Re: Mankind
11/17/93 8:57 a.m.

My zen-like gram got panned the other day, so here is something worldly to contemplate:

From 1850 to 1925, all the information in the world doubled (seventy-five years).
From 1925 to 1950, it doubled again (twenty-five years).
From 1950 to 1970, it doubled again (twenty years).
From 1970 to 1985, it doubled again (fifteen years).
From 1985 to 1995, it will triple (ten years).

Are we conducting business the same way we did in 1985? Are we keeping pace? Are our systems keeping pace? What can we do differently? I'd very much like your insights.

To: All Katz Managers and Sellers
From: Bob McCurdy
Re: Service
11/23/93 8:40 a.m.

Providing outstanding service to both clients and agencies is now the price of admission to stay in business. We know we have truly accomplished legendary service when our clients or buyers talk about what we did and the outstanding service we have provided. Service is about hustle just as rebounding and defense is about hustle in basketball. It is all about desire. People talk about the legends in sports, movies, or music all the time. We should strive to put forth one legendary servicing or sales effort daily.

If we do this, we too will become legends, the legends of radio.

To: All Katz Managers
From: Bob McCurdy
Re: Training
12/2/93 9:07 a.m.

I always thought one of the best things about training someone is that it forced me to get better at the things I am teaching. Teaching or training others requires the teachers to improve first, which is a good thing. Training is not only for the newly hired. How are you training your experienced sellers to get them to the next level? Weekly? Individually? Train, and you will force yourself to get better. There is only one thing more exhilarating than teaching and learning, and that is selling, the more the better.

One of your most important jobs is to make all around you better.

To: All Katz Employees
From: Bob McCurdy
Re: Feedback
12/2/93 8:56 a.m.

I'd like your input and feedback. If you were the president of Katz, what three things would be your highest priorities in 1994?

Please be honest and say what comes to mind. If you are concerned about confidentiality, fax or send your thoughts to Elissa. Take it from me. She is tight-lipped. The people who sit next to me on the train talk to me more than she does.

Express exactly what is on your mind minus any expletives. If I can take Liz Haban's assistant calling me Bobaroni, I can take anything.

Thanks.

To: All Katz Employees
From: Bob McCurdy
Re: 3 Priorities
12/13/93 11:19 a.m.

About a week ago, I sent out a radiogram requesting your thoughts regarding the three major priorities facing this company in the coming year. Let me phrase it this way, the response to date to my request is less than the turnout for a town "selectman" election during a winter blizzard.

    Things are winding down a bit. You do have some time. Share your thinking. Thanks!

To: All Katz Managers and Sellers
From: Bob McCurdy
Re: Distinction
12/10/93 9:12 a.m.

Every interaction we have with someone personally or professionally is an opportunity for distinction. I don't think we ever want to just think of ourselves as average. The reason we have embraced our expectations is our distain for the mediocre. Every day there are numerous opportunities for distinction, which is simply going "above and beyond" what's expected. Let's not let daily opportunities for distinction pass us by.

    Have a great weekend, and make it distinguished!

To: All Katz Managers and Sellers
From: Bob McCurdy
Re: West Palm Beach
1/10/94 1:41 p.m.

Something happened to us that hasn't happened in two years—we got fired. WOLL FM made the determination that their national sales interests would be better served by another company. Our billing was up this year. Our share was up this year, but they still felt that a change would benefit them.

The loss of their $300,000 in billing will not make or break us, but this should serve as a wakeup call. Life is about cycles, and the cycle of Katz dominating Interep will not change immediately. Great companies rise to the challenge to meet power with more power, skill with even more skill, and desire with even more desire.

Take a minute to reflect upon what we could have done differently. Sometimes a loss is good, but it is only good if we learn from it and take great pains to ensure it doesn't happen again. We are not invincible. May I recommend that it might be time to redouble our efforts to deliver clients with legendary performance and service.

To: All Katz Managers and Sellers
From: Bob McCurdy
Re: Success
12/13/93 8:26 a.m.

Over the years I've developed a guiding principle that has come in handy, and it's based upon this … one of the few things in life people would rather give than take is advice. When I am faced with a dilemma, and I am not sure what my response should be, I ask myself, "What would I suggest to someone on my team to do if they were in the same situation." It kind of simplifies and distances me from the problem. This process allows me to give me advice, and you can't not follow your own advice, right? The best way to succeed in business and life is to act upon the advice you'd give to others. Advice, we give it by the pound and take it by the grain, but take your own.

To: All Katz Managers and Sellers
From: Bob McCurdy
Re: KLOS Los Angeles
1/18/94 9:16 a.m.

Please take a minute to review this. You might keep it handy before handling a Los Angeles opportunity.

KLOS is a tough sell right now. We are rationalizing, looking for sympathy about how difficult of a sell this station is now. But sympathy is like junk food—it provides no real nourishment, and it is not good for you. We can't be content with giving it a good try. We can't give ourselves permission to lose, which all but guarantees a loss. Rise to the challenge, get me involved, don't lose alone. Be at your best. Be angry, be determined, but don't be accepting with anything other than a KLOS order.

To: All Katz Managers and Sellers
From: Bob McCurdy
Re: Words of Wisdom
5/10/94 7:40 a.m.

"The secret to your future is hidden in your daily routine." This is an old New Guinean proverb. What we do today and how we do it determines where we go and how much we make. Initiate and don't react. How can you better refine your daily routine? What's your routine on the weekend? It's a great time to get ahead of the pack at your own pace.

"What you fail to master will eventually master you." This one is Hindu. If we are honest with ourselves, we don't need managers to tell us where to improve. Become your own improvement engine.

Finally, there's, "You will never possess what you are unwilling to pursue." This one is American. Go out and grab what you want. Deserve it. Work for it. Winners don't wait for the ship to come to shore. They swim out to it.

Be the best you can be every day.

To: The Future Stars of the KRG
From: Bob McCurdy
Re: Listen
6/23/94 6:56 a.m.

You usually hear that a person talks too much, never that they listen too much.

Let your buyers talk.

Let them finish their thoughts without interruption.

Listen intently.

The more they talk, the more you'll know how to sell them.

How do you feel about someone who you believe is not interested in what you have to say?

Don't be worried about your response. Listening intently will tell you how to respond.

People like to talk, especially about themselves. It makes them feel good. People like people who make them feel good … and people don't do business with people they don't like.

If you don't listen intently, you will miss the real objection.

Take notes.

Remember, two-thirds of communication is nonverbal. It is not what you say but how you say it.

Listening is a skill all of us can work on. Being the life of the party and extremely vocal is not always the best thing. Did any of you write any of the above down yesterday in our meeting?

To: All KRG Trainees
From: Bob McCurdy
RE: The Weekend
6/24/94 1:45 p.m.

The weekend is here. How are you going to be better on Monday? There are seventeen of you in this program; which of you guys are going to become the future leaders of this company? Remember, your own individual actions or inactions determine your success and professional security.

Being in this program is quite an honor. You were not hired to be average or good salespeople; you were hired to redefine excellence in this company. If we wanted good or average sellers, we wouldn't be spending $15,000 each to train you. We are expecting you to live up to the performance history of the KRG and continually striving for excellence, which is what this company is about. Excellence is voluntary. How good do you want to become? Be the best group of training graduates, ever. Hustle.

To: All Katz Managers and Sellers
From: Bob McCurdy
Re: Being a Pro
9/20/94 7:13 a.m.

Came across this quote that hit home. "A professional is someone who can do his/her best work when he/she doesn't feel like it."

We all have days when we're "on," and we all have days when we'd rather be anywhere else but in the office. It's the challenge of being at your best when you prefer not to. The key to keeping Katz, Katz, is to always gut it out and do what we know we should be doing. This requires a tremendous amount of discipline. The "best" realize that no matter what the circumstances, they owe it to themselves and their coworkers to always be at their best.

Have a great day.

To: All Katz Managers
From: Bob McCurdy
Re: Leadership
10/1/94 8:57 a.m.

Be less concerned about improving your management skills. I believe people would rather work for a leader than a manager. Rarely is passion associated with a manager. Rarely is passion *not* associated with a leader. You manage things; you lead people. Do we inspire them? Do they respect us? Are we making them better? Do they see the sacrifices we are making to make them better? Are we the proper role model? Are we making them feel proud to be part of this company? To be working for us? I kid about the inverted pyramid around here, but the fact is if they work for you, you now work for them. They have to feel so darned good about working for you and what you stand for that they could never imagine working for someone else.

To: All Katz Managers and Sellers
From: Bob McCurdy
Re: Four-Minute Mile
5/11/95 8:12 p.m.

Came across an article about Roger Bannister, the first man who ran a sub-four-minute mile. It was interesting in that scientists at the time were looking for physiological reasons why it was impossible for humans to run that fast. Their logic was flawed, thinking just because it was never done it that it was impossible.

The reason why others were soon able to do what Bannister had done was due to their beliefs changing. When one's beliefs about limits change, the limits themselves change. Belief leads to reality.

Who among us is leading the charge to accomplish the "impossible"? Who among us has mastered leadership? Management? New biz development?

In our own way, we can be the equivalent of Roger Bannister in the radio world. The powerful thing is that once one person shows something is possible, others will follow. Lead us to make the impossible possible.

To: All Katz Trainees
From: Bob McCurdy
Re: Hunger
5/13/95 4:08 p.m.

I just read a competitor's press release touting the promotion of two sellers to VP/sales. I used to love calling against these types of sellers. They have been in the business for a dozen years. Their commitment to improvement has waned. Their focus due to other interests has become less intense. They are rarely on the cutting edge of where this business is going. In their own minds, they are legends.

It is these types of sellers who are vulnerable to aggressive, dedicated, focused, and ever-learning young salespeople. Salespeople who are eager to leave their mark on the industry. Sellers who are eager to move up in the company.

I know there is no way that a dedicated, aggressive, and less experience sales executive doesn't outperform an older, more complacent seller, but this only happens if the less experienced seller is committed to daily improvement and possesses constructive dissatisfaction.

This is the exact reason why we began and continue the training program—to outperform those experienced who have "arrived" in their own minds.

To: All Katz Managers and Sellers
From: Bob McCurdy
Re: Essence
5/17/95 7:50 p.m.

Several times in the past few weeks, we have discussed the importance of understanding the "essence" of what a client station stands for. It's about what makes it unique and special.

What's the "essence" of Katz? It is simply this: We've got a bunch of people who take a tremendous amount of pride in their work. They are dedicated to excellence, and they don't stop until they get the job done. The "essence" of Katz is we love a good fight and hate to lose.

There are a bunch of other rep companies that would like to taste what it would be like to be #1. If we keep living the essence of this company, we'll keep them wistful for a long time to come. Remember, ability gets you to the top, but character keeps you there.

We are a bunch of old-fashioned working stiffs with character. A successful past doesn't mean a successful future, so onward with vigor.

To: All Katz Managers and Sellers
From: Bob McCurdy
Re: Larry King
5/19/95 7:13 a.m.

This will take the form of a Larry King Column.

➢ It seems like we can be doing a better job of communicating the buying criteria to our station contacts.
➢ It seems as if we could be more responsive to sensitive clients who are experiencing billing issues.
➢ It seems as if we could be doing a better job of helping in the development of our younger sellers.
➢ It seems as if we could know our station sales strategies more deeply and thoroughly than we do.
➢ It seems as if the assistants can do a better job of answering the phones.
➢ It seems as if we could provide the assistants with better leadership and guidance.

These were some of the things dancing through my head coming in on the train this morning. If you have any suggestions or feedback, it would be most appreciated. Have a great weekend.

To: All Katz Managers and Sellers
From: Bob McCurdy
Re: Solicitation
5/23/95 3:10 p.m.

Just got off the phone trying to close a new client. Solicitation is a long-drawn-out process, as it is not easy to get a station to fire their current rep.

This makes me appreciate all the more the wonderful and lengthy list of clients that we represent. It would be impossible to re-create this list of stations today, and if you could, it would require several lifetimes. Just as the pyramids were built one block at a time, this company has been built one station at a time, and we sell one station at a time. We are now sitting at the top of this pyramid, and we need to make sure we stay there.

I say to young folks trying to break into the industry that they must "respect" the industry. I say to all of us that for us to continue to be the best we must respect all of the hard work and effort by all of the previous Katz employees over the years that had a hand in building this Katz juggernaut.

To: All Katz Managers
From: Bob McCurdy
Re: Job
5/26/95 7:36 a.m.

A key role of any manager is identifying talent. While doing so, make sure you are not being too critical. Jerry West of the Los Angeles Lakers is a great judge of talent because he can see what the player is today but also envision what he can become. Make sure you are not being too critical. Have high expectations and even higher standards, but focus on if that individual has greatness within them. In hoops, the scouts look for speed, quickness, jumping ability, and attitude. We should be looking for desire, attitude, likeability, and work ethic. We have hired some green, green, green trainees that have turned out to be something special. So be cognizant to look beyond the individual who is sitting in front of you and project what they can become with the proper, training, management, and leadership.

To: All Katz Rising Stars
From: Bob McCurdy
Re: Enthusiasm
6/2/95 11:16 a.m.

Every person is enthusiastic about something in their lives. Some get enthusiastic for ten minutes, some for ten weeks, but it is those who remain enthusiastic about their livelihood throughout their career that become true stars.

We've talked about "essence" recently. What is there not to be enthusiastic about this job? You work for a great company with great people and role models. You are paid a fair wage, and you can just learn, learn, learn.

It is nobody else's job but your own to keep your enthusiasm candle burning. Don't ever let the simple "wins" and little things about this business that you like so much ever fade. Maintain this enthusiasm, and you will become a star!

To: All Katz Managers and Sellers
From: Bob McCurdy
Re: You
6/3/95 11:26 a.m.

Keep in mind that it is our own individual actions that determine our success and not the judgments of others. It's what you do and don't do that will make a difference. It is usually the individual who remains focused, works it hard, and takes responsibility for his or her own actions that rises to the top. There are no politics in this company.

I chose Katz over Blair fifteen years ago, as I believed at Katz if I did what I had to do and did it well, I would get due recognition. I have found this to be true. Remember there is no future in any job. The future lies in the person holding it.

Be yourselves and understand that we are committed to performance and client satisfaction. Those that do a better job in these areas will be given additional responsibilities.

To: All Katz Rising Stars
From: Bob McCurdy
Re: Ready
6/4/95 9:31 a.m.

In life, business, and sports you must be ready when your opportunity comes along. History and business are full of characters who were ready to rise to the occasion. Where would the Houston Rockets be if Sam Cassell, a bench player, didn't rise to the occasion?

The point is you must be prepared to come off the bench and contribute. Every company goes through turnover for one reason or another, but when it happens, you need to be prepared to step in and assume additional responsibility.

When you rise to the challenge, your self-esteem will grow. Your perception inside the company and within the industry will grow, and you put yourself in the position for more responsibility.

Expect the unexpected. Approach each day as if it might be the one that thrusts you into the limelight.

You owe this to your coworkers, and you owe this to the company. It's a great feeling to be needed, and you are needed now, but there will be a time when we will really need you—be ready! Thanks.

To: All Katz Managers and Sellers
From: Bob McCurdy
Re: Singleness
6/4/95 5:10 p.m.

I read something in the bio of Gandhi the other day, and it referenced something called the "singleness of decision." What he meant by that was that life was difficult enough and that we'd just bring additional stress to ourselves if we had to go through a decision-making process every time we were faced with a decision.

This "singleness of decision" is applicable in business. Whenever I am in town, regardless of the time I got home the previous evening, I will be on a certain train in the morning. It doesn't matter what the agenda is for the weekend, I will find time to study and improve myself.

"Singleness of decision" requires discipline and the courage to make a stand. Making a commitment to improve over the weekend is as natural to me as going to church. I wouldn't blow off church, and I will not blow off time for self-improvement. There is no equivocation about this.

"Singleness of decision" serves those well who are able to maintain it.

To: All Katz Rising Stars
From: Bob McCurdy
Re: Remember
6/5/95 9:44 a.m.

As sure as I am writing this, each of you will get job offers, next month, next year, the year after. I was talking to a recent training program graduate recently when she said, "You know, it is really unbelievable how attractive we become to other companies once they find out we came out of the Katz training program; it's amazing."

You have received the best training in the business. You are managed and lead by industry pros, you have probably developed more discipline and worked it harder than you ever have or thought you ever would.

The point is this. You are part of something special here and that we recognize that you are special and for Katz to remain on top we must employ great people. You fit the bill—if you continue to work hard.

What I'd like you to do right now is think of all of the great stuff you've learned, the great people you've learned from, and the privilege of being with the best.

Remember how thrilled you were to get the job offer from this company. Remember how thrilled you were to graduate from the training program. Remember how thrilled you were to get your first account list.

Etch them in your mind and never forget this company made this possible. It is a "double loyalty" kind of thing. We will always do all within our power to lead in an ethical manner and be worthy of your loyalty. All we ask is for your loyalty in return.

Ingrain these thoughts in your mind so when the inevitable job offers from other reps and radio companies come, take a second to think about the above. There is honor in being loyal. It separates the great from the good.

To: All Katz Managers
From: Bob McCurdy
Re: Improve
6/6/95 6:39 a.m.

Each day we should be asking ourselves what did we do to make our stronger performers stronger. What happens in public education is too much time is spent on the slower performers and not enough with the exceptionally bright.

How are you challenging your exceptional performers to improve? The individuals are the future divisional VPs, presidents, and GSMs of the company. Plus, these are the individuals who are most attractive to the competition; they tend to be less patient and want to learn and want to grow. It is in our self-interest to comply.

At the same time, ask yourself if you are doing what's necessary to get rid of the weaker performers. The company is only as strong as its weakest link. The more strong performers we have, the stronger we'll be. And getting rid of a weak link gives us the opportunity to hire a strong performer.

Getting rid of the weaker performers puts more responsibility on you to train, etc. Accept this willingly. Sometimes it is not the people you fire but the ones you don't but should that provide the most headaches.

Focus on developing the exceptional talent and get great replacements for those who can't become better than mid-tier. We owe it to each other to do this.

To: All Katz Managers and Sellers
From: Bob McCurdy
Re: Compartmentalize
6/8/95 8:04 a.m.

You know how once in a while in sports you see a player lose his cool after making a turnover, foul, error, or mistake, and what he does after the mistake is worse than the mistake itself. The ability to compartmentalize is important.

The great salespeople, businesspeople, doctors, athletes, and lawyers are able to contain something negative and not let it impact them moving forward. It takes a lot of discipline and composure to master compartmentalization.

If we had a difficult call with a client or buyer, instead of letting it impact what you do next, take a deep breath, have your assistant take a message if you are not "ready" for the next call, go for a walk around the office or block. But don't allow a blown sale or negative conversation to negatively impact your next call.

It is easier to say than do. Wipe it clean from your short-term memory. Smile before you pick up the next call. There is nothing worse than shooting yourself in the foot as goodness knows, there are enough people out there shooting at us.

Compartmentalize, you will be glad you did.

To: All Katz Managers and Sellers
From: Bob McCurdy
Re: Managing
6/13/95 7:00 a.m.

The homily at my Mass dealt with the trinity in the Catholic Church, which is the Father, Son, and Holy Ghost. These three entities comprise God for us Catholics. That's a pretty heavy concept to fathom, but it got me thinking, as managers we need to be three people every day.

A manager: Making sure that we get the things done that should be done. That the office runs smoothly.

A leader: Setting the pace, direction, and tone of the office. Establishing a vision of where you believe the office should be headed and communicating this vision to your sellers.

An enforcer: Making sure whatever is not going the way it should, gets fixed. It means having the difficult conversations. It means challenging the sellers to improve. It means setting demanding and challenging expectations, and it means not backing off them.

Lastly, there were no potential sellers at Mass. I checked.

To: All Katz Managers and Sellers
From: Bob McCurdy
Re: WSJ
6/14/95 7:37 a.m.

This morning in the WSJ there was an article dealing with the importance and impact various CEOs' parents had on them.

There were some interesting comments regarding the teaching of discipline, role models, taskmasters, perseverance, etc.

Every one of them stated that their parents were the most important reason they developed the attitudes and principles they did.

The point of this radiogram is hello, Mom; hello, Dad. As managers for ten hours a day, we fit the role of parent for our teams. Even if you don't have biological kids, you have "kids."

Develop, develop, develop them. Just as in the family where the parents exert the most powerful influence over their offspring, it is also true at the office.

To: All Katz Senior Sellers
From: Bob McCurdy
Re: Leadership
6/17/95 8:55 p.m.

One thing about Pat Riley's resignation from the Knicks that was of interest was his comment that no one from the players ranks stepped up to push the players. It had to be someone who had the player's respect, and this individual had to be one of if not the team's star. When Riley was with the Lakers, he had Magic Johnson step up to lead the other players. This did not happen with the Knicks.

For us to maintain our lead over the competition, we need you senior sellers to step up and lead by example, support the manager, and point out to the manager what he or she should be doing. Be the eyes and ears for the manager. Adopt a rookie and get involved with their training. Mike Agovino and the Divisional VPs fill this role for me. They have saved me from making many dumb decisions.

Be sure to give your managers this kind of feedback and be sure to set the example to which the younger sellers aspire.

You will find your job to be even more rewarding and the company better if you embrace this role and responsibility.

To: All Katz Managers and Sellers
From: Bob McCurdy
Re: Required
7/5/95 9:01 a.m.

There are times when doing all we can to close a sale is enough. There are times though when doing our best is not enough, and we must do what's required. There is a difference. "Required" deals with actual performance, no excuses, goal accomplished. "Our best" deals with effort.

There are requirements for greatness and continued success. Sometimes "best efforts" need to be elevated to another performance plateau. Giving our "best effort" psychologically gives us an "out" if we don't achieve our goal. Doing what's required give us no alternative and no "out."

The "required" can be consistently accomplished if we keep the gap between how we do our jobs and how we know how to do our jobs as narrow as possible.

The rep that "does" and performs at the higher level more

consistently and skillfully will prosper. Deregulation is coming. Let's widen the gap between Katz and the rest of them to put ourselves in a position of continued success.

To: All Katz Managers and Sellers
From: Bob McCurdy
Re: Theory
7/7/95 7:40 a.m.

I was talking to a client yesterday who was trying to dissect what made Katz, Katz.

At first, he concluded it was a theory. A set of beliefs and maxims that if followed would lead to what Katz had become. A road map, if you will.

He then stated that maybe it was "performance." Katz was Katz because of its performance. Our reputation was developed and self-perpetuating.

He then felt that that wasn't definitive enough. He then said Katz was Katz due to its sellers. We hire the best sellers, so it was only logical that they outperform the competition.

At this point I am sitting back smiling trying to figure where he's going to end it.

"No," he said. I think its Katz's upper management. Five or six strong managers who "will" the company to perform.

We then drifted to another topic.

The fact is Katz is all these things.

Our theory is a sound one, one that's based upon hustle, knowledge, and a strong set of values.

Kats is Katz due to performance—we compete, and we never stop selling.

Katz is about great salespeople and sales management. You can't win a war without the best soldier and leaders.

There is no secret to Katz. Every day each of us plays a very important part in making sure the effectiveness of this company is unleashed to the benefit of our clients and ourselves. Every single one of us plays an important role in keeping this Katz "theory," or whatever it is, moving forward.

Have a great day!

To: All Katz Managers and Sellers
From: Bob McCurdy
Re: Future
7/11/95 7:57 a.m.

If there is one thing that become increasingly clear to me the more time I spend in this business, it is that every little thing I do or don't do each day comes back somewhere down the road to either haunt or help me.

In this regard, we're a lot like farmers. The guy who farms when he feels like it is not likely to produce a banner crop.

What we are now is a direct result of what we did in the past. The future is nothing more than a bunch of "nows" that have passed. The future can't help but be a reflection of what we've done and the value we put on our "nows." No way around it, we are the sum total of our choices we have made and continue to make daily.

What's the future? It is nothing more than an approaching bunch of "nows." Our future will only get brighter if each of us make better use of the current moment.

To: All Katz Managers and Sellers
From: Bob McCurdy
Re: Uncomfortable
7/13/95 7:32 a.m.

A good question to ask ourselves is how we can make ourselves uncomfortable today, and I am not referring to losing a piece of business we should have closed.

If we are too comfortable, it means we probably aren't growing enough. If we stick to what we mastered, we'll never get better.

I always like when I get a little apprehensive about something. It makes me work harder; I get better prepared, and I get more focused. And the best part about it is that after I've done it, I feel good about myself.

Exposing yourself to the uncomfortable keeps you fresh and professionally alive. It is the best preventive medicine for burnout that I know of. World records are not broken by people in comfort zones. The best understand this and act upon it, shunning too much comfort.

To: All Katz Managers and Sellers
From: Bob McCurdy
Re: Fundamentals
7/21/95 6:39 a.m.

Sometimes I think the greatest ability of a salesperson is to approach each day as if it is their first. I think the tendency to let up a bit or to cut a corner here and there is as natural as eating, breathing, or sleeping.

This tendency to assume that a selling situation will unfold in a certain manner is as powerful as gravity, so is the tendency to choose what fundamentals we'll employ on each avail due to circumstances could result in us leaving dollars on the table.

Experience is good from the standpoint that it fine-tunes our intuition, but it could be harmful if we allow ourselves to project the future based upon past successes.

Selling is like shaving. No matter how well you did it yesterday, you got to do it all over again tomorrow in the same focused fashion otherwise risk getting nicked.

I guess it might be said unlearning certain aspects of our past successes could be a big contributor to future successes.

To: All Katz Managers and Sellers
From: Bob McCurdy
Re: #1
7/18/95 12:15 p.m.

The higher you climb, the more you become exposed. Make no mistake about it; what we have, every one of our competitors wants. As Trout & Reis said, the only thing that can bring down the market leader is the market leader. Commitment to the basics will ensure that we don't become our own worst enemy.

We should be flattered that the Christal President, Bill Fortenbaugh, was quoted in the latest issue of *Radio Ink* saying that they believe they can replace us as the #1 rep. We welcome the challenge.

The bottom line is that we have got to want to stay on top more than our competitors want to topple us. It is that simple and that difficult.

Every minute we are not doing what we should be doing, we are allowing a competitor to inch a little closer to that #1 ranking.

We all understand the quality of a person's life is in direct proportion to their commitment to excellence. We all need to be bound at the hip in this belief.

To: All Katz Rising Stars
From: Bob McCurdy
Re: Responsibility
7/19/95 7:24 a.m.

With the good fortune of joining the #1 national rep comes responsibility. The responsibility of perpetuating this success—the privilege of keeping this company great. It is something that can't be taken lightly.

You are the future of this place. You and your action will determine if we remain on top for years to come.

Responsibility means tough decisions, long hours, and doing things others shun doing.

You are part of something special here. We appreciate your support, loyalty, and dedication. At some point, you will have the opportunity to pass on this legacy. That is pretty cool!

To: All Katz Managers and Sellers
From: Bob McCurdy
Re: Negotiate with yourself
7/26/95 7:08 a.m.

Everyone wants to feel good about themselves and the job they have done. We set our own definition of a good job either consciously or unconsciously, and the tendency might be to set it too low so that when it is all said and done, we feel good about ourselves and the job we've done. Who doesn't want to feel good about themselves? Self-esteem is critically important.

Every sales opportunity, before we negotiate with the buyer and before we pick up the phone to talk to our client, we've likely already had some kind of internal negotiation with ourselves to identify what is a good job. That's only human.

I'd venture to say those in business who limit or hold in check their self-negotiation and set their bar a little higher tend to rise quicker.

To: All Katz Managers
From: Bob McCurdy
Re: Leadership
8/10/95 9:32 a.m.

➢ Is being there when they need you.
➢ Committing your own sweat first.
➢ Doing what you expect them to do.
➢ Giving consistent and honest feedback.
➢ Behaving as a role model.
➢ Carrying yourself with dignity.
➢ Setting high expectations.
➢ Mastering your trade. An airtight commitment to self-improvement.
➢ Putting the needs of your team and the company ahead of yours.
➢ Disciplining when discipline is necessary.
➢ Oozing integrity.
➢ Recognizing the importance of being respected first and liked second.
➢ A leader's job is getting great work from good people.

Just a little reminder this hot summer morning.

To: All Katz Senior Sellers
From: Bob McCurdy
Re: Toughness
8/11/95 1:46 p.m.

All of the top performers possess it. Few can stay on top without it. This trait is every bit as important as it has always been.

Toughness doesn't mean being belligerent. Rather it is a steadfast focus with tact. It is doing what you might not want to do but doing it anyway. It is not rolling over in the face of a challenge. It is standing toe-to-toe with a buyer and diplomatically defending and selling the value of your station. It is having the competition realize they are in for a battle if they tangle with you or one of your stations.

Toughness doesn't mean we still can't be perceived as fun, nice, and likeable. On the contrary, combine toughness with being fun, nice, and likeable, and you will be unbeatable.

Toughness is hanging on to what you have worked so hard to achieve while the rest of the world tries like crazy to pry it away.

Toughness is recognizing what it takes to remain the best and then doing it.

Thanks for all of your toughness, and have a great weekend.

To: All Katz Managers and Sellers
From: Bob McCurdy
Re: Parkinson's Law
8/12/95 10:21 a.m.

As you know from Mike's email, business is starting to slow down. Does that mean we have to slow down? When things are crazy, we all wish we had more time to do all the things we know we should be doing. It seems that many of us might have this time now.

Now is the time to catch our breath, but it also the time for us to create our future and create our own luck. Hustle as much now as when business was booming except you will be doing more seeding for the future. Parkinson's law states that work expands to fill the time available for it. Let's avoid this trap. Let our competitors nap while they wait for the phones to ring.

Use this time to presell, build upon your relationships, and devise ways to get a higher share on the next opportunity. Only you know if you are being as productive as you can be. What does your "internal" voice say?

To: All Katz Managers
From: Bob McCurdy
Re: The Katz Difference
8/14/95 2:32 p.m.

It all boils down to performance. What kind of share do you think our competitors would do if they had our resources and client list? What kind of job do you think any of the KRG companies would do?

What kind of job would we do with their client list? Would we increase revenue 5 percent, 10 percent, 20 percent? Would we even increase it?

The single most important factor in your office's performance is your expectations. Sellers rarely reach their potential with no other role model than themselves. You are a stretch inducer.

Is our current success a function of us or our client list? If a company is as good as it has ever been, it will never become a has-been. Are we as good as we have ever been? Something to think about.

To: All Katz Managers and Sellers
From: Bob McCurdy
Re: Realistic
8/18/95 11:44 a.m.

How many times have you heard the phrase "get real" or "let's get realistic" or "come on."

Maybe sometimes we are better off by not being realistic. We might accomplish more. Maybe we put limits on ourselves by being realistic.

What great feats have ever been accomplished by anyone who is realistic? Realistic implies ordinary. If it is currently "real," it is in existence, which means a lot of other people are already doing it.

We are not being paid to be realistic. Our reputation has been made on delivering the unexpected sale, which requires us being unrealistic.

Realistic implies being reasonable. Great sellers, leaders, or companies don't get that way by imposing reasonable expectations upon themselves and their staffs. They are reasonably unreasonable.

Let the competition be realistic and reasonable. When it comes to performance and judgment of that performance, let's continue to be reasonably unrealistic. It will continue to provide us with a slight edge.

To: All Katz Managers
From: Bob McCurdy
Re: Model
8/21/95 7:23 a.m.

People rarely improve when they have no other role model but themselves. We have sixteen sellers on the staff with less than one year of experience. I don't see this as a negative; I view it as an opportunity to develop some outstanding stars of the future. But they will only become stars if you model the type of behavior and standards that you expect of your team every day.

People don't approach the ideal where the ideal doesn't exist or takes days off. Stretch daily!

To: All Katz Rising Stars
From: Bob McCurdy
Re: Work/Play
8/24/95 7:25 a.m.

Came across this: "The master of the art of living makes little distinction between his work and his play, his labor and leisure. He might hardly know which is which. He simply pursues a vision of excellence at whatever he does leaving others to decide whether he is working or playing. To him, he's always doing both."—James Michener

You know when I was on vacation earlier this month, I was getting ribbing about my emails and how I should just lay back and relax. Well, I did a lot of that too, but I was also relaxing when I was answering or responding to emails because sometimes I can't tell the difference between working or playing. I know some of you feel the same way. May the rest of the world be as lucky.

To: All Katz Managers and Sellers
From: Bob McCurdy
Re: Sovereign
8/28/95 8:05 a.m.

Interesting quote in *Forbes* this morning: "The obligation of the subjects to the sovereign is understood to last as long, but no longer, than the power of the sovereign is able to protect them."

In today's business environment it could be translated to mean that as managers, we will have the loyalty of our people so long as we are able to assist them in achieving their career goals, assist them in improving, be available to them and come to their assistance when they need us, and always put their needs and well-being before our own.

If we don't do this, just as with the sovereign, they will find someone else who will.

To: All Katz Managers and Sellers
From: Bob McCurdy
Re: Have to
9/4/95 12:55 p.m.

There is a big difference between "have to" and "want to." "Have to" is related to rules and guidelines. It connotes something negative if something isn't done. It implies less than 100 percent buy-in on the doer's part. It often leads to doing something just to get it out of the way. Excellence is rarely a by-product of "have to."

"Wanting to" do something is powerful. "Wanting to" do something is based upon the existence of a goal and the understanding of short-term sacrifice in return for long-term success.

There are certain tasks we might not really "want to" do, but we do them anyway as we are in pursuit of a goal. People with the "have to" mentality might just punt it and leave the task undone.

Great companies have more people who "want to" than "have to." Much of it boils down to perception, attitudes, and goals.

To: All Katz Managers and Sellers
From: Bob McCurdy
Re: Success
9/17/95 2:05 p.m.

Many business books make it to the top of the charts bought by people looking for some magical advice. The following advice is not magical, but it will help you succeed. It is a surefire way to put your careers on the fast track and blow past the competition, and that is to work it as hard on Friday as you do on Tuesdays and Wednesdays. The nice thing about this is that you don't need to spend one more minute in the office.

Teams that don't play hard from the time the whistle blows to the final buzzer sounds rarely become champions. Hustle might just be one of the most important skills to possess.

To: All Katz Managers and Sellers
From: Bob McCurdy
Re: Stimulation
9/28/95 7:14 a.m.

The other night I caught an interview with a football coach whose team had just lost a game they should have won. It was a big game and a very disappointing loss. In response to the question, "How does it feel to lose this game?" the coach's response was that it "stimulated" him. He clearly was disappointed, but he was resolute to do something about it.

We all experience disappointing losses from time to time—business that we should have won. Maybe our response should be one of stimulation, to win back what is rightly ours. My guess is that stimulation will get us to the feeling of exhilaration when we close the order— the exhilarating feeling that comes from a job well done.

To: All Katz Managers and Sellers
From: Bob McCurdy
Re: Dictionary
9/11/95 7:43 a.m.

Was helping one of my kids look up some definitions for a homework assignment. One of the words he needed to check out was "tragedy."

I'll give you my definition of tragedy. It is when some individual at some point in their life looks back and says, "I should have, I could have, or I wish I had."

We not only owe it to ourselves to be the best of which we are capable of becoming, we owe it to our spouses and our children. Your career, expectations, and performance have the potential to positively impact many, many people over your career.

Let's make sure woulda, shoulda, coulda doesn't come back to haunt us.

"Twenty years from now you will be more disappointed by the things that you didn't do than by the things you did do. So throw off the bowlines. Sail away from the safe harbor. Catch the trade winds in your sails. Dream. Discover."—Mark Twain

Good selling!

To: All Katz Managers and Sellers
From: Bob McCurdy
Re: 5 minutes
9/22/95 7:22 a.m.

I was watching a football game the other day, and one team had a comfortable lead, but the other team came roaring back. The game got close, the intensity increased, and everyone on the field was finally giving it their all.

The one thing that always amazed me was how professionals

allowed their efforts to ebb and flow. I have seen the same thing with salespeople. Sometimes they believe their lack of effort no longer matters, and they will still succeed anyway. Those that fall into this trap set themselves up for an unpleasant fall.

The great salesperson approaches each day and every avail with the urgency and intensity of there only being five minutes left in a game.

To: All Katz Managers and Sellers
From: Bob McCurdy
Re: Watch out
10/6/95 7:46 a.m.

In the next few weeks, we will be in the second phase of "watch out" months. We got out of the first phase of "watch out" months with the passing of the summer.

They are "watch out" months because it is easy to get distracted with all of the holidays and festivities. It is key that we finish the year strong, and that means hustling all twelve months. No one that I know of ever won a mile race by running three-quarters of a mile, no matter how fast they ran it.

This is the time of year that actually works to our advantage, while the others "chill out," we'll be "watching out."

To: All Katz Managers and Sellers
From: Bob McCurdy
Re: Role Players
10/12/95 7:23 a.m.

Someone came into my office the other day and mentioned the importance of having role players. I responded that it "depends."

If I am coaching baseball, I might want a player who could play multiple positions reasonably well or be a great fielder but poor hitter. If I am a Hollywood producer, I might want a great character actor to support a great leading actor.

When it comes to selling, though, I don't believe we should be content with role players. In sales, the definition of excellence is someone who can take over any agency, handle any client, and assume more responsibility in time of need.

We don't need role players who can only get along with certain types of buyers, not be able to handle certain agencies, only handle small volume, and not be projectable to step up in time of need. We are shunning our responsibilities if we accept this.

Think about this and think about your people. We will remain Katz if we have role players and not stars.

To: All Katz Managers and Sellers
From: Bob McCurdy
Re: Dislikes
10/16/95 7:37 a.m.

Do you like getting up at 5:00 a.m.? Would you rather sleep until 6:00 a.m.? Do you enjoy making a sales call at 5:00 p.m., or would you rather wait until the next day? Do you enjoy studying your trade or would you rather watch TV? Do you enjoy getting up in front of a roomful of people, or would you rather sit back? Do you enjoy planning your day, or would you rather wing it? Do you prefer dealing with media buyers, or would you rather deal with planners?

Make no mistake about it, people in general have very similar likes and dislikes. The difference is that those who succeed overcome their dislike of some things and then consistently do them.

If I have learned anything the past twenty years, it is that those who succeed subordinate their dislike for something and do it if they know it will make them more effective professionals.

You can question this conclusion, attack it, and kick it around, but it is a common denominator of success.

To: All Katz Managers and Sellers
From: Bob McCurdy
Re: Habits
10/18/95 7:11 a.m.

There are good ones and bad ones and ones we don't even know exist. What habits should you consider altering? Habits are silent. They are as automatic as blinking and breathing because they are so ingrained in our routine.

I think I'd be safe to say that we'd all become a little bit better if we bring to the forefront some habits and begin to evaluate them. There is a good chance they might not be serving us the way they originally did.

To: All Katz Rising Stars
From: Bob McCurdy
Re: Resistance
10/19/95 7:24 a.m.

Flashes of brilliance won't do it. A great presentation won't do it. A great personality won't do it. Dressing sharp won't do it.

The best antidote to resistance that I have come across is persistence. Sometimes we succeed when we don't have the sense to quit. Persistence is by far the main ingredient for closing the great sale.

What are you being persistent about today that will lead to a great sale? If you are persistent today, it will end up being a good day. If not, you have some unfinished business.

To: All Katz Managers and Sellers
From: Bob McCurdy
Re: Champions
10/30/95 7:31 a.m.

I got a little emotional reading this to our managers this week at our managers meeting. I wrote it in about ten minutes. It was easy to compose as it is all about who you are.

Champions:

> ➤ Do what others don't like to do not because they enjoy doing it but because they know it must be done.
> ➤ Meet every challenge head-on offering no excuses regardless of outcome.
> ➤ Understand that nothing of value can be accomplished without discipline.
> ➤ Accept, embrace, and welcome the responsibility that comes with being #1.
> ➤ Understand that being significant requires sacrifice.
> ➤ Have a stronger commitment to the fundamentals than the competition.
> ➤ Act like they have been there before when they close a big sale.
> ➤ Understand that persistence wins.
> ➤ Respect all unless otherwise earned.
> ➤ Possess a deep confidence in their abilities, which are built upon a foundation of preparation.
> ➤ Recognize there will always be imposters who are trying to take what they have.
> ➤ Understand that they can never not lead.
> ➤ Relish the fact that they will be held to a higher standard of performance and would never want it any other way.
> ➤ Come closest to maximizing their God-given ability.

➤ Possess integrity, which is simply the value they place on themselves.
➤ Are not afraid to have to reprove themselves every day.
➤ Do it better than it has ever been done previously.
➤ Work at Katz.

Everyone take a bow. I have been here for fifteen years, and the talent level has never been stronger. My thanks to you all.

CHAPTER 9

The Beasley Years

Happiness is working with great people.

—Unknown

W hat follows are Beasley Sunday memos from 2017 to 2020 sent to Beasley sales management. They are a little longer than my Katz ones, as I only wrote them weekly. It is uncanny how similar the topics were.

Each week I tried to share with the Beasley sales management staff thoughts that they could share and discuss with their teams. Unlike my previous positions, the Beasley sales management teams did not report directly to me, so from a "tone" standpoint they did differ somewhat from my earlier Katz communication.

As with the previous communication, the following appears as sent out originally.

To: All Beasley Sales Managers
From: Bob McCurdy
11-19-17
Re: Leadership

I pulled the following from a deck delivered almost a quarter century ago when speaking at a client's managers meeting.

Thought it might a worthwhile share as we prepare to outperform in 2018. The fundamentals simply do not change.

Leadership: The most overlooked ingredient to sustained success.

We all focus on the mechanics of running a sales staff.

How much time do we set aside to master our leadership skills?

What are your expectations?

Can you quickly rattle them off?

Have you taken the time to write them down?

Have you communicated them to your staff?

Great leaders:

➢ Make the difficult decisions when they need to be made.

➢ Understand the importance of constantly upgrading their staff. Doing otherwise is an affront to those performing.

➢ Commit their own sweat before they commit their people's.

➢ Recognize and welcome that their actions are scrutinized, understanding that at times wordless leadership by example is the most effective leadership.

➢ Flawlessly model expected behavior.

➢ Understand that they can't improve others until they begin to improve themselves.

➢ Quickly admit mistakes.

> ➢ Are considered to be extremely knowledgeable by their staff, yet they recognize how much more they need to learn and then do something about it.
> ➢ Understand that they "protect" their staff and their family's future by pushing their teams hard.
> ➢ Are not afraid to induce positive tension.
> ➢ Earn trust by putting their people's interests ahead of their own—every time.
> ➢ Have the courage to make unpopular decisions.
> ➢ Understand that to master the art of leadership they must also master the art of followership. To become a great leader, they understand they must also be a great follower.
> ➢ Must have a bias for action.
> ➢ Never allow their people to grow old in their jobs. They reinvigorate and elevate.
> ➢ Are their organizations' accelerator.
> ➢ Have a reliable and constantly refined sense of true north.
> ➢ Operate as a "water boy" to their people.
> ➢ Possess a deep belief in their cause. Understand they will not inspire others to follow unless they possess absolute conviction.
> ➢ Never pass up an opportunity to teach.
> ➢ Possess three key "bones"—the funny bone, the wishbone, and a backbone.
> ➢ Consistently get great work from good people.
> ➢ Are constantly challenging their staff and themselves to narrow the gap between what they are accomplishing and what they are capable of accomplishing.
> ➢ Set the standard for excellence in their companies.
> ➢ Look beyond themselves, their market, their company, and their industry in setting standards and expectations.

> ➤ Are selfless and understand that the only things they can truly "keep" are the things they can "give away"—skills, values, expertise, their knowledge, etc.
> ➤ Understand that there is no greater gift than having the opportunity to positively impact their team's careers and lives.

What kind of leader are you?

How would you describe yourself? Honestly.

Would you like to work for you?

Where do you really compare against in-market peers? Industry peers?

How can you improve? What are you waiting for?

Leadership is about the basics:

Dogged commitment to core values.

Complete honesty and transparency.

Being in the trenches boosts morale more dramatically than any incentive program.

Giving the staff something that they can't get anywhere else.

Do not hesitate to tell us what you and your team need to make both happen! Let's end '17 strong while building upon '18's pace.

To: All Beasley Sales Managers
From: Bob McCurdy
12-12-17
Re: Leadership

Came across an interesting "leadership" article in *Forbes* earlier this week. There is also a survey link within the article, which if clicked on will provide with a better understanding of your individual leadership style. Click here for the article and the survey link within the article. Well worth five minutes to take the survey.

Leadership fundamentals do not change. The thoughts below were taken from notes taken in the '80s.

Leaders:

> ➤ Lead. There are no statues of committees in any parks. No one follows a committee into battle.
> ➤ Understand that the bottom 20 percent holds them back and replaces them. No company has all As and Bs, and the definition of what constitutes As and Bs needs to rise every year to effectively compete.
> ➤ Are servants to their teams and its greater "cause."
> ➤ Recognize that there are no mature industries, only tied imaginations.
> ➤ Master "creative overkill," communicating the same message in multiple, creative ways.
> ➤ Buy into the fact that one individual with courage makes a majority.
> ➤ Realize they must go to extremes in matters of principle, developing no moral callouses.
> ➤ Are comfortable inducing positive tension.
> ➤ Embrace the belief that there are no bad soldiers only bad captains.

➤ Elevate all around them.

➤ Are comfortable that their high-performing team is a good place to work but not an "easy" place to work, due to performance expectations.

➤ Believe it is a leader's job is to identify talent, attract/hire the talent, train the talent, bring that talent to its fullest potential, seamlessly integrate the talent into the team, and then keep that talent on the team.

➤ Understand their team is a reflection of their expectations. The measure of leadership is not the quality of the head but the tone of the body. Are the people reaching their potential?

➤ Are realistic but still expect the impossible.

➤ Avoid spending too much time on the inside so they maintain in touch with the outside.

➤ Are cognizant that a company managed in a normal way with normal expectations will produce average results.

Have a terrific and productive week!

To: All Beasley Sales Managers
From: Bob McCurdy
12-26-17
Re: Successful People

There was interesting article that touched on what it takes to succeed. An excerpt:

> Success in life does not come easy. It is fraught with pitfalls, obstacles, failure, and mistakes. Success requires persistence, mental toughness and emotional toughness in overcoming these pitfalls. Its pursuit pushes you to the edge emotionally and

physically. You must become accustomed to struggle
if you hope to succeed.

In short, the successful become mentally tough, which creates a solid foundation for long-term success. Successful people are great at delaying gratification (overcoming oneself in some way). They are also great at overcoming fear in order to do what they need to do. That does not mean they are not afraid/concerned; it does mean they have the courage to overcome their fears/concerns and do what they know should be done.

Successful people also consistently do what is important, asking themselves constantly throughout the day if what they are involved in will help them achieve their goals.

And successful people never forget that "school" is really never out, understanding that it's what they learn after they know it all that really counts. Successful people are lifelong learners. They have taken control of their lives due to them having taken control of their own learning.

All of us, and our sales teams, need to exhibit this persistence, mental toughness, and penchant for learning as we enter 2018. A personal reexamination of how we each approach our professional responsibilities and a commitment to expand upon that definition will go a long way toward all of us achieving our personal and corporate goals.

Thank you for all of your efforts. Everyone starts at "go" in a week.

To: All Beasley Sales Managers
From: Bob McCurdy
12-31-17
Re: Attitude

The week of relaxing, reflection, and re-energizing is over, and it is game time; the first inning of a twelve-inning game begins in twenty-four hours.

We have sixty-four "work days" to nail down one-quarter of our 2018 budget, so it has to be all hands on deck—from the get-go. It is key that the entire Beasley team hit the streets running 8:30 a.m. on Tuesday.

Let the competition "ease" into the year on Tuesday morning, rehashing their holidays. We need to be all business, and as sales leaders, we can reinforce this message and set the tone for the next twelve months, come Tuesday a.m.

Have never seen those with a laser-like sense of urgency **not** outperform those without one.

It is not enough for us to aspire, desire, dream, hope, or intend to make 2018's budget; it must become our "crusade" to make 2018 budget. If it is our "crusade" as the company's sales leaders, it will become our team's "crusade" as well.

Thomas Jefferson once said, "Nothing can stop the man/woman with the right mental attitude from achieving their goal; nothing on earth can help the person with the wrong mental attitude."

Stated differently, collectively, it is our attitude that determines our revenue altitude.

I dug out a book by Charles Handy titled *The Age of Paradox*. A recent discussion with A. J. Lurie brought it back to mind. Some interesting parallels remain almost twenty-five years later:

> Life will be unreasonable in the sense that it won't go on as it used to; we shall have to make things

happen for us rather than wait for them to happen to us.

Many want "more of the same," but, unfortunately, that is seldom possible.

What worked well last time around will likely not work as well the next time.

Some want to prolong the old ways indefinitely and fail. Others search for the "new" and succeed.

The world belongs to the discontented.

Enough is never enough until you have "exhausted" all of your potential. (Love this one.)

If we all "exhaust" our potential in the coming year, it will be a year to remember.

Let's collectively make 2018 the year of Beasley!

To: All Beasley Sales Managers
From: Bob McCurdy
1-28-2018
Re: Attitude

A good friend, Don Jacobs, who oversees Townsquare's Sioux Falls cluster, recommended a book titled *Obvious Adams*, written in 1915 about an ad man who continually gets promoted by acting upon the "obvious." It is available on Amazon for $6.95.

My initial thinking was how good could a book that cost six bucks be, and when it arrived, it was so unimpressive in both length and appearance my first inclination was to just toss it aside unread.

But there was something about the word "obvious" in its title that kept resonating. A couple of days later I picked it up and read it in about thirty minutes—it's only forty-two pages.

I have read hundreds of business books over the years, but this one was surprisingly thought provoking in its simplicity.

While driving from Tampa to Fort Myers earlier this week, the book and word *obvious* came to mind again after listening to Jim Croce sing about the "obvious" in that you don't:

> tug on superman's cape,
> spit into the wind,
> pull the mask off that old Lone Ranger,
> and you don't mess around with Jim.

When the song was over, I began to think about what was "obvious" about sales and revenue in our industry and the "obvious" actions required to continue to prosper. I came up with a baker's dozen. I am sure you can easily come up with more. I only focused on sales. There surely are an equal number of "obvious" issues and "obvious" solutions pertaining to programming.

It is obvious that:

➤ The sophistication required to succeed in sales will only increase.
➤ Long term we need to become more of a "digital" company than a radio company.
➤ If we do not acquire new skills and change, slightly declining revenue could be the "good old days."
➤ The importance of providing compelling cross-platform marketing solutions is now table stakes.
➤ Like it or not, data and analytics will continue to grow in importance. The data genie is not going back into its bottle.

➢ There will be more audio competition, not less, in the months and years to come.

➢ Competition for the local ad dollar is going to increase, as will the number of media vendors vying for local advertisers' time and attention.

➢ Double digit radio revenue increases are not on the horizon any time soon.

➢ Business development will only increase in importance.

➢ The equation more time selling = more $$ generated, will not change.

➢ Simply competing against other radio broadcasters will not increase industry revenue.

➢ In this era of collective ADD, sixty-second commercials are simply too long. The migration to shorter-length commercial messaging would benefit both advertiser as well as the station.

Once we identify the "obvious" challenges, the actions to address them become "obvious," not any easier, but more manageable. It is obvious that we need to:

➢ Embrace digital, data, and Biz Dev with tenacity.

➢ Recognize that our local sales success will increasingly depend upon our cross-platform solutions.

➢ Begin to think and act more like marketers with the goal of becoming our clients' sustaining marketing resource.

➢ Identify a way to spend more time outside the office in front of clients. The "absent" are usually forgotten and rarely sought.

➢ Remain learners. There's the "know it all" and the "learn it all." We need to be the later.

The "obvious" is often extremely difficult to resolve and execute, but how we react and address the "obvious" will determine the brightness of our future.

While at times the sheer magnitude of what is "obvious" and its difficulty might appear to be overwhelming, once compartmentalized, it becomes infinitely manageable. While it made sound trite and overly simplified, if we all commit to execute and perfect the "obvious," the best revenue days are ahead of us.

To: All Beasley Sales Managers
From: Bob McCurdy
1-27-18
RE: Don't Belong

"I don't belong here."

I am reading a book recounting Muhammad Ali's first fight with Joe Frazier in 1971, which was labeled "fight of the century."

Late in the fight, Ali was knocked to the canvas for the first time in his career, at which time he appeared to have already lost the fight. When asked afterward why he had gotten up, Ali responded, "The first thing I heard was "eight" and then the first thing I thought was that I don't belong here." He then got up off the canvas and finished the fight. In spite of him losing this bout, he was still a champion, and as Ali said, current or past champions do not belong on the ground. For Ali it was about pride.

The two fighters met twice more in the ring, with Ali winning both fights.

So where do we, Beasley's Best, not "belong"?

The first thing that comes to mind is that we "don't belong" pacing behind last year, as we have more going for us in terms of staffing, resources, and sales tools than we had January 2017.

The second thing that comes to mind is that we "don't belong" missing budget.

The good news is that both are not cut in stone, and we have two months left to accomplish both. A couple of things to ask ourselves:

Are we investing enough time training our newer hires? Double and triple team them. They are our future.

Are we getting in front of the economic decision-makers with enough compelling ideas that move their business forward?

We all know we "belong" at budget; now it is up to all of us to make it happen. Nailing down Q1 puts us in a good position for making 2018's. It is about pride of performance and doing what we know can and should be accomplished.

Thanks for all your efforts.

To: All Beasley Sales Managers
From: Bob McCurdy
3-18-18
Re: Teach

Are we finding a way to put our up-and-coming new talent in situations where they can really spread their wings, to find out just how good they can be? To determine if they have superstar potential.

Do we each have enough up-and-coming talent on our staffs? Young talents whom we believe have the potential to become As with the right kind of guidance and coaching. If not, we need to find them and hire them. They are not easy to find, but find them we must. It is easily one of our most important responsibilities. Staffing our teams with the right talent takes a back seat to no other responsibility.

A staff comprised of the strong talent does not guarantee that our staffs meet budget and outperform the market, but no staff without strong talent has the chance of doing so.

Are our C players preventing us from giving this up-and-coming talent an opportunity simply because these Cs have been around for a while, have a good month every now and then, usually perform when they know they are on the hot seat?

Are we losing or discouraging some talent with big upside due to an inability to grow and being "blocked" by Cs?

Cs are not our future. High potential up-and-comers are. It is imperative we nurture their development and train them.

To: All Beasley Sales Managers
From: Bob McCurdy
4-29-18
Re: Doing Differently

It's April 29, 2018. The year is already one-third of the way over and a good time for a "checkup."

We all move pretty quickly with a lot on our plates, but our business is not really different from any other in 2018.

How are each of us approaching our jobs differently thus far '18 versus '17? Have we spent any time thinking about this question? Acted upon our answers?

If asked this question could each of us provide specifics? If we asked our salespeople, could they? Are they approaching their jobs differently? Are we? Is it apparent to each of our sales teams how the '18 version of ourselves has morphed and is more effective than the '17 version?

The end of April is not a bad time to reflect and act upon our answers to these questions.

All of us moving in the same direction with the same sense of urgency will get us to where we want to be.

To: All Beasley Sales Managers
From: Bob McCurdy
5-16-18
Re: The FWMUS Trap

Just like a speed trap, we all fall into this trap at one time or another. It is a trap that leads to less than optimum performance. As leaders, it is not only our job to avoid this trap ourselves, but we need assist our sales staffs to navigate around it as well. It can sneak up quickly and can kill an entire quarter or even a career.

The FWMUS trap is also known as the "Forgot What Made Us Successful" trap, and it starts by taking shortcuts and selectively executing the fundamentals when convenient.

The best way to avoid this trap is to:

➢ Never take for granted that we "belong" or will always "belong." In business, the only way we truly "arrive" is when we retire.

➢ Defiantly commit ourselves to a tougher standard of learning and performance. Establishing performance levels below which we collectively refuse to go.

➢ Operate as if each day was the first day on the job.

➢ Understand that excellence is the gradual result of always seeking to do better. It is a habit. Not an act.

➢ Recognize when we stop getting better, we stop being good. Keenly aware that the skills that go us to where we are will not be enough to keep us there.

➢ Buy into and relish the fact that success is never final.

➢ Conquer complacency.

➢ Be disciplined. Discipline like any other skill can be refined and honed.

We continue to chip away at last year's pace. You guys know what needs to be done and how to do it.

To: All Beasley Sales Managers
From: Bob McCurdy
5-12-18
Re: Success

There is no secret to success. As much as we would like, there just is not a magic bullet. A couple of "rounds" that touch on what it takes to succeed were in an article this weekend in the *Wall Street Journal* by Peggy Noonan titled "Wisdom of a Non-Idiot Billionaire." In it, she discussed the philosophy of Ken Langone, founder of the Home Depot. Some of what she touched on follows.

*You teach values by living them. People absorb *eloquent* action.

> That is a great phrase—eloquent action. What eloquent, sublime, groundbreaking actions, activities, or changes have we each individually undertaken recently that serve to elevate the expectations of our staffs of themselves.

*Pray at the feet of hard work. Be ravenous in reading about your field, whichever you wind up in and for however long.

> No one ever sat their way to success. This quote from tennis great Rod Laver says it all: "People ask why I train so much and work so hard. Well the answer is simple: I will not allow somebody with twice the genetics and half the determination be better than me."

Regarding ravenous reading about our field. An old UCLA coach once said to me "reading is listening." It took me a while to get it, but I got it. We all have the opportunity to "listen" to the smartest people who ever lived by reading about them, their writings, and their teachings.

We have the opportunity via blogs, articles, and books to "listen" to the brightest in marketing and advertising minds and put their teachings to work for our clients—every day. There is something highly noble about the continued pursuit to narrow the gap between what we are accomplishing and what we are capable of accomplishing.

*Stay excited. Don't be sated.

This is the most exciting time I can remember since I got into this business in 1976. Have always believed the way to be safe professionally is to never be sated professionally. We all have to keep this great industry growing for the next generation of broadcasters and the generation after that.

*Admit the reality around you, than change it.

GE's ex-Chairman Jack Welsh used to say, "Look reality in the eye and act on it—fast." A while back I wrote a blog titled "It's Obvious" taken from a book titled *Obvious Adams*. We all know what needs to be done; now we have to do it. To do otherwise is to short-change ourselves.

We are halfway through the quarter. It would be a good time to conduct a one-on-one with each salesperson and do a deep dive on their account list to identify any accounts that we might be able to move over the top yet in Q2. Any accounts that we might have overlooked, any accounts that should be reassigned, any accounts that might benefit from a client workshop, any accounts that we could interest in digital, etc.

Account-by-account excellence + avail-by-avail excellence + AE-by-AE excellence + managerial excellence = budget.

It all starts with some eloquent action on our part.

To: All Beasley Sales Managers
5-31-18
Re: The More Things Change, the More They Don't

Was going through some old notes this weekend from 1991.

Had saved them so figured might as well read them. Was kind of like delving into a time capsule. It was clearly a crazy time with a deep recession in full force. A couple of things stood out:

➢ The battle for controlling "costs" is never ending.
➢ The pursuit for the right operating structure is ongoing.
➢ What is already known by the older generation becomes "new" and the rage to the current generation.
➢ Predictions are usually wrong. Network TV and ad agencies were supposed to be long extinct by now.
➢ The need for managerial audacity continues.
➢ The fundamentals of leadership don't change.

A few quotes from various business leaders in 1991, almost three decades ago, that are as applicable today as they were when stated:

➢ You don't change things forever with the same old song and dance.

➢ Any company that hesitates to attack itself usually loses market share and market leadership.

➢ Today, people who can "think" are exceptionally valuable.

➢ Tomorrow's winners are those who remember to make their selling efforts bolder, nimbler, and more opportunistic than ever.

➢ Radio is still a great business; just need to have the right cost structure.

➢ Smart businesspeople don't wait for a trend to be obvious to act on it.

➢ Nothing as demoralizing as a boss who tolerates second-class work.

➢ Exert unremitting pressure on the professionalism of our staffs.

➢ Hire people smaller than you will become a company of dwarfs.

➢ Raise your sights, blaze new trails, and compete with the immortals.

➢ Better at discrediting the old than designing the new.

➢ Can't manage by nostalgia.

One blurb I had copied from an article that year rings as true today as it did then:

> Every major industry was once a growth industry. The reason it atrophies is due to the failure of management. What previously successful industries lacked was not opportunity, but the imaginativeness that made them great in the first place. To survive you need to plot for obsolescence of what now produces the majority of your revenue. Because of

their hesitation and unwillingness to pioneer the future previously successful industries are now faced with new, aggressive competitors and obsolescence.

Clearly, the more things change, the more they stay the same. Previous generations of radio leaders were equal to their respective challenges. So must we.

To: All Beasley Sales Managers
From: Bob McCurdy
6-24-18
Re: Stretching

Stretching is the only way we grow, individually or as a company.

Stretching is narrowing the gap between what we are currently accomplishing vs. what we are capable of accomplishing, knowing the difference, and acting upon that difference.

Stretching is doing the things we know we should be doing but do not want to or have decided not to do.

Stretching is not accepting procrastination.

Stretching is attacking some aspect of our job that where we (not necessarily our managers) know we need to improve.

Stretching is continually reinforcing a "stretch" message to our staffs and getting them to embrace professional growth. Every one of us should be six months better today than we were at the end of '17.

Stretching often hurts. Extending ourselves is not easy, but it enables us to go a bit further today and even further tomorrow, as the benefits of stretching compound.

Stretching is a skill all peak performers have developed in their careers.

We have got some stretching to do, but we have the team in place to make it happen!

To: All Beasley Sales Managers
From: Bob McCurdy
7-28-18
Re: Stand Apart

Those that stand apart:

- ➢ Do what they said they would do when they said they would do it.
- ➢ Do what is expected <u>and</u> then some. There is rarely a traffic jam on the road to "above and beyond."
- ➢ Continually seek to refine their craft.
- ➢ Look the part. Understand that first impressions are last impressions.
- ➢ Zig when everyone else is zagging. The herd is often wrong.
- ➢ Become active participants in their own "rescue." Fully embrace, "If it's to be, it's up to me."
- ➢ Seek to improve oneself before expecting others to improve.
- ➢ Believe that there is a chance that the other guy just might be right.
- ➢ Listen intently.
- ➢ Evaluate and pause before responding.
- ➢ Seek first to understand and not immediately assess.
- ➢ Have inoculated themselves against the NIHS syndrome (not invented here syndrome).
- ➢ Have the courage to retain conviction in the face of resistance. Recognize that all new ideas and suggestions typically go through the three states of ROSE—ridicule, opposition and then self-evidence.
- ➢ Seek to influence the company and peers beyond their current title/role.
- ➢ Behave as if everything they do and say will be on the 6:00 p.m. news.

- ➢ Don't poke holes in the proposed solutions of others but seek to also find solutions.
- ➢ Find a "way" or makes one.
- ➢ Often ask, "Why not?"
- ➢ Understand that the one who quits last usually wins. It is always too early to quit.
- ➢ Understand that excellence is the result of gradual improvement.
- ➢ Realize that when it comes to performance and tasks, it is not about "or" but the genius of "and."
- ➢ Embrace the fact that you do not truly take control of your own career until you take control of your own learning.
- ➢ Allocate some portion of their weekend to getting ahead of the Joneses.
- ➢ Buy into the fact that the fundamentals don't change; what changes is our attention to them.
- ➢ Believe the status quo should be broken.

Read a book this weekend whose last line was, "working together in concert, you can transform your business virtually overnight." It was written 102 years ago. While I question if we can change our business overnight, there is little doubt that together we can transform our business.

Make it a great week.

To: All Beasley Sales Managers
From: Bob McCurdy
12-30-18
Re: Everyone Needs a Coach

A doctor in a Ted talk was talking about the importance of one of our most important jobs—coaching our people, which also includes coaching and challenging our best performers, some of whom have been doing the job for decades, some of whom might not want coaching. In fact, these salespeople probably require our coaching as much if not more than anyone.

Quotes from the video:

"You are never done. Everyone needs a coach. The greatest in the world needs a coach."

Michael Jordan, LeBron James, Tom Brady all have had coaches who challenged them to improve and work on weaknesses. We should think of ourselves as coaches, not merely managers, as our most important job is developing our people. If we develop our people, budgets will be the result.

"Pay someone to come into my operating room to observe me and critique me."

Our people do not need to pay anyone. They have us. Get out on the streets with them, observe them, and provide feedback as to how they might improve.

"Expertise means not needing to be coached."

Clearly incorrect, which the doctor acknowledges—expertise in any field is a constantly evolving thing. In business we never "arrive"; there is always another challenge, which requires enhanced expertise to overcome. In business and sports, those who are *not* effectively coached inevitably lose to those that are.

"You don't recognize the issues that are standing in your way, or if you do, you don't necessarily know how to fix them, and somewhere along the way you stop improving."

When improvement stops, professional decline begins. None of the skills that got us to where we are today can keep us there. The great coach of the San Francisco 49ers, Bill Walsh, said, "The biggest room in the world is the room for improvement." A room in which all of us reside.

"It was a whole other level of awareness."

You can't improve without knowing where you need to improve.

Delegate some of the tasks that keep you behind the desk and get out on calls with your team to provide that "awareness."

"He was describing what great coaches do, and what they do is they are your external eyes and ears providing a more accurate picture of your reality."

We can provide our salespeople with the unbiased benefit of our insights. It is a win-win for all involved.

"I think it's not how good you are now; I think it's about how good you are going to be."

The great performers narrow the gap each day between what and who they are versus what they are capable of becoming. Great coaches are able to assist their salespeople to embrace a vision, stretch themselves, getting comfortable with being uncomfortable, while opening their eyes to new opportunities and possibilities.

The best coaches are creative masters of overkill. Being able to communicate the same message in a new and different way to each salesperson and have them welcome the messaging. The best coaches also realize that to make themselves better, they first have to improve themselves and work diligently to do so.

As we head into 2019, let's reflect upon our sales teams and how we might coach them to even greater things next year.

There is something noble about assisting our teams to be their best—personally and professionally. That is about as good a definition of "success" as there is.

While we attempt to make this happen, we should keep in mind we will always encounter some twists and turns, but that is okay.

A good coach may take people where they want to go, but a great coach takes them where they do not necessarily want to go but ought to be.

See you in 2019!

To: All Beasley Sales Managers
From: Bob McCurdy
2-10-19
Re: Lunge

Years ago, I developed the habit of cutting and pasting quotes and retaining interesting ways a thought or idea was phrased. For me, they often serve to clarify and get me thinking about a topic or subject in a different light.

I came across this one; I might have previously referenced it, but it is one of my favorites: "Don't just lean into, but lunge at it."

"Leaning into" communicates more of a restrained, toe-in-the-water, tepid interest or effort, something less than an all-out commitment. It is better than not leaning but will likely result in middling results.

On the other hand, "lunging" at some task or challenge, communicates being "all in," a head-first dive, a total commitment, and vigorous assault on an obstacle or opportunity. Lunging at the right stuff has the potential to produce outstanding accomplishments.

Everyone involved in Beasley revenue generation should always be lunging at something revenue related:

As managers, it is our job to identify the "right stuff" at which our staffs should be lunging, hopefully in unison, coaching, encouraging, and cajoling them to make the plunge. Outstanding performance more often than not will be the result.

It is too competitive to just lean. Those that succeed moving forward need to all-out lunge.

Make it a great week.

To: All Beasley Sales Managers
From: Bob McCurdy
3-3-19
RE: Urgency

A sense of urgency. It is good to have one. Those that close more sales possess one. Those that make budgets possess one. Those who identify, attract, and hire the best sales talent possess one. Those who have thriving, evolving, and enduring careers possess one. Those who are capable of maintaining it most consistently throughout their careers usually retire with the larger bank account.

A sense of urgency is about consistent, proactive action not reaction. A necessary sense of urgency is about approaching our responsibilities at a consistently challenging pace that constantly "stretches," is sustainable over the long term, yet does not overwhelm.

Over the years it has always bewildered me how some salespeople have been able to rediscover a sense of urgency when management turned up the "heat." Peak performers, on the other hand, have usually developed the habit of creating their own "heat." And while they might ultimately be able to "refine" a thing or two about their job approach, rediscovering a sense of urgency would not be one of them as operating at a challenging, self-imposed pace is second nature.

Business has slowed for March and Q2. It is critical that all on our teams approach their responsibilities with a sense of urgency, stretching professionally with every sales tool and sales angle employed. In this sluggish revenue environment, we can afford no expectations.

Note, managing with a sense of urgency does not imply the need to invoke anxiety, fear, of panic. It is simply about creating an environment in which *complacency* is absent.

Was listening to WFAN this morning, and they were interviewing the University of Pittsburgh hoop coach. He said something interesting. "Leadership is all about creating a culture, and a culture is all about creating habits, and habits reflect accepted and expected behavior." Leadership-culture-behavior-habits-urgency.

Make it a great week!

To: All Beasley Sales Managers
From: Bob McCurdy
3-24-19
Re: Comfort Zone

One of our GSM's in Detroit sent me a chart last week after my meeting with the Detroit staff about the importance of "stretch," taking advantage of our digital assets, and approaching our responsibilities in an enthusiastic, ever-evolving fashion.

Take a minute to review. If any of our salespeople remain in the "comfort zone," it is on us. It is simply incumbent upon us to make it uncomfortable for anyone to remain in a comfort zone.

Too many, based upon our digital sales revenue, appear to be residing in either the "comfort zone" or "fear zone." These individuals, in some cases, have been selling radio for a decade or longer, often handle the largest lists and see the radio world changing under their feet as it gets more digitally and data focused. These salespeople must understand that more of the same, in terms of approach, will deliver more of the same, which will not get us to where we need to be and cannot be acceptable.

It is in the "fear zone" and "comfort zone" where the excuses flow like the Mississippi. If we accept them, it is on us. Effective leaders get people to do what they might not exactly want to do but should be doing. All involved with revenue generation should either be in the "learning" or "growth" zone.

It has never been implied that we turn any on our staff into human nerve endings, but it has been suggested, often, that we take a velvet glove approach—make it clear that certain behaviors are expected. We need to gradually tighten the grip until the salespeople recognize we are not going away, and they will not be able to talk their way out of altering their behavior.

To: All Beasley Sales Managers
From: Bob McCurdy
4-29-19
Re: Smarter

Brian Beasley shot me this article. Thought it was totally on point. Took the liberty of editorializing/customizing it a bit with some "comments" regarding the article's key topics. Enjoy the day!

Mental Strength

Comment:_Developing mental strength is a work in progress. Intelligence is a work in progress. Everything a smart person knows, he or she learned from somewhere at one point or another. Getting smarter does not necessarily mean a huge commitment of time and energy every day. If you can consistently train your brain to adapt to new situations and information, you will get smarter with time.

Reading Is Insanely Essential

Comment: It is not only reading all the industry trades but keeping the important stuff that we read handy for future reference.

Embrace Lifelong Learning

Comment:_If we don't learn something new every day that we can use and repurpose professionally the rest of our career, do so before our heads hit the pillow each night. As Warren Buffet said, "The more you learn, the more you earn."

Subscribe to Insightful Newsletters

Comment: Some might cost a few bucks like *AdWeek*, *Ad Age*, *Automotive News*, etc., but the best investment anyone can make in their career is an investment in their own professional knowledge. Each buck invested pays back hundredfold over a career. That is a good return on investment.

Create Value

Comment: Be worth being "seen." The way to be worth being "seen" is to be visible with value, and the best way to bring value is to know your business and their business cold. Smart, focused people bring value. Smart is not just about IQ but preparation and study.

Take Notes

Comment: Stash away any and all facts, data, quotes, paragraphs, blogs, articles, etc., that you believe have the ability to assist you in better making your case with a client today, tomorrow, or a year from now. Think long term. It is better to overdo it with notes than underdoing it. You can always delete some stuff later. Conversely, it is extremely difficult to find the stuff you did not keep that you now could use. This is within all of our control.

Share What You Learn

Comment: The only things in life we can truly keep are things we give away, and that includes knowledge. Share what you learn with your peers and clients. Establish yourself as *the* expert in your building and ad community. Elevate others through your presence and make them better. Extend your influence beyond your title. Publish what you learn in your market or beyond. Writing will help you organize your thoughts. It's one of the reasons I write the Saturday blog. It forces me to formalize my thoughts on key topics, and in the process, I learn while hopefully positively impacting others and positioning myself with clients, a win-win-win.

Reflect

Comment: Reflection is a big part of learning. An experience is not truly ours until we digested it, reflected upon it, and finally understand it. Honest reflection without rationalization.

Cultivate Self-Awareness

Comment: Emotional intelligence. What kind of impact are we having on the people with whom we interact? Read unspoken body language closely. Continually test your "gut" so you have more confidence in it moving forward. Throw out "trial balloons" in the form of questions to get a better handle on your impact on the person to whom you are speaking. What is *not* said is often more important than what is said. Know yourself. This is not easy. Understand yourself. This is not easy. Need to do that before we can truly understand others.

Compete with Yourself

Comment: John Wooden, when he was coach of UCLA, always said never compare yourself to others, as you have no control over them. Focus within. Success in business and life comes from consistently working to narrow the gap between what we are currently accomplishing vs. what we are capable of accomplishing. Seek to narrow this gap daily, and you will have succeeded when it is all said-and-done, whenever that may be.

All Worthwhile Things Require Effort

Comment: President Calvin Coolidge said, "There is no development physically or intellectually without effort, and effort means work." We become successful because we worked hard, but often the tendency is to work less hard the more successful we become, thus putting our hard-earned success at risk. Do not trust professional happiness and don't forget to continue doing what got you to this great party. Treat each day as if it were your first day on the job.

If You Want Long-Term Success, Stop Avoiding What Is Hard

Comment: Embrace what is hard while the competition avoids it. If it were easy, everyone would be doing it or already have it. Do the unrequired. All things are difficult before they become easy.

Make it a great week!

To: All Beasley Sales Managers
From: Bob McCurdy
5-5-19
Re: One More

One of anything is typically no big deal. One cent. Can't buy much. One bite. Not enough. One pushup. So what. One sock. A problem. One potato chip. Impossible. One swig. Still thirsty.

But there's transformational power when "one" is something that is done consistently by many.

Think, we would generate more revenue if all 230 of us Beasley sales managers and salespeople made a commitment moving forward, each day to:

make one more new biz call,

or

make one more face call,
>   or

send out one more pre-sell piece,
>   or

touch base with one more client,
>   or

write one more thank-you note,
>   or

learn one more thing that can used the rest of a career,
>   or

discuss our digital assets with one more client,
>   or

line up one client workshop,
>   or

deepen our relationship with one more key decision maker,
>   or

reach out to one key decision-maker with whom we have no relationship.

Is it beyond our capacity to commit to do *any* of the above one additional time daily through the end of '19? Don't think so.

There are 160 workdays left in 2019. Multiply this figure by 230 of us, and that equals 36,800 of the above, which we would not have done had we not consciously committed to doing "one" more each day; 36,800 of something is a lot of anything, but 36,800 more of above spells success.

Before wrapping up our day, ask ourselves if we have done "one additional," and if not, do so before jumping in the car. Doing so every other day would still be 18,400.

If we *all* make this "one" commitment, in spite of what Three

Dog Night once sang, one will *not* be the loneliest number, and as Queen sang, we'll be "the champions."

To: All Beasley Sales Managers
From: Bob McCurdy
7-1-19
Re: Constraints

Every business has constraints. There are all kinds: economic, structural, regulatory, personnel, expertise, etc.

The two constraints that are totally within our control are "vision" and the "will" to make that vision a reality.

Great performers and companies are flexible enough and adept enough to meet goals in spite of these constraints. They look reality in the eye and act accordingly.

Are we producing corporate revenue goals in spite of these constraints? Not currently.

Are the fundamentals that have impeded our ability to meet these revenue goals likely to change? Not likely.

We have a choice. Continue along the path of missing revenue goals and watch our revenue continue to shrink or begin developing other meaningful revenue streams. Unlike the Stones who sang "Time Is on My Side" in 1964, it is no longer on ours.

General Douglas MacArthur famously said, "The history of the failure of war can almost be summed up in two words: "too late."

> ➢ Too late in comprehending the deadly purpose of a potential enemy.
> ➢ Too late in realizing the mortal danger.
> ➢ Too late in preparedness.
> ➢ Too late in uniting all possible forces for resistance.

Our role as leaders in this company is to address difficult decisions head-on. We have decisions to make now, as it is not too late—until it is, but the window in which to make these decisions is closing fast.

Internet ad spend will have grown five times faster than traditional media spend over the last decade.

Our revenue performance won't be unacceptable to us until it is— and then it will be too late, as change will then be thrust upon all of us, and out of our control.

If we want to remain relevant, we have to be willing to reevaluate all that we do and how we do it and take some risk. It is a good time to solve this puzzle.

To: All Beasley Sales Managers
From: Bob McCurdy
7-14-19
Re: Mediocre

Interesting perspective from an article I came across recently.

John Allert, who has been CMO at McLaren for well over a decade, explained that while the business enjoys a fierce rivalry with Ferrari, its true nemesis comes in another form: mediocrity.

> Our nemesis—the thing that worries us most—is letting down ourselves and the premise of our brand through mediocre performances, errors, faults, or even just doing something that's seen as being average. We are effectively allergic to mediocrity, and there are all sorts of checks and balances to try to mitigate against that ever happening. The thing that could undo us the most is not our competition— it is mediocrity.

McLaren's nemesis of mediocrity keeps the business honest and focused on what matters most. Like the phrase "allergic to mediocrity" as well as "letting ourselves down."

Is it possible for us to achieve our potential with C and D sales talent? Grade your sales team on a ten-point scale and not on a curve. Be sure that if you give them a 10, they would be a 10 in any one of our markets.

Any organization is only as strong as its weakest links, and it is virtually impossible to make budgets held back by Cs or less.

In the current revenue environment, it is not unrealistic to state that each cluster's sales staff would need to average somewhere close to a 9 to nail budget.

Is it possible to make budget with a staff that has several Cs or lower? It might have been in the old days or with powerful revenue tailwinds, but those gusts have all but turned into zephyrs at best. Any Cs or lower competing against a competitor's As or Bs results in lost revenue.

As managers, we establish performance criteria below which we refuse to allow our salespeople to function. Anyone who is not a B player or above needs to understand that immediate improvement is required. If they are engaged and active participants in their own improvement, we will give them some additional time to turn it around, with the operative word being *some*.

Beasley has 181 salespeople across our markets, excluding managers and digital execs. Are all Bs or higher? You don't bring a knife to a gunfight, and you don't make challenging budgets in a tepid revenue environment without top talent. This is within our control and responsibility as managers. We owe it to each other to make it happen.

Alexander the Mediocre surely did not make history.

To: All Beasley Sales Managers
From: Bob McCurdy
8-17-19
Re: In Search of Better

In search of better. I came across these four words in a Seth Godin blog recently, and they really hit home. The subject of self-improvement has intrigued me my entire career. These four words encapsulate the actualization process of becoming what we are capable of becoming, both personally and professionally.

In 1982, Tom Peters was also "searching" when he wrote the book *In Search of Excellence*, which was a huge best seller. Is the search for "excellence" and the search for "better" the same thing? Close, but not quite. "Excellence" is defined as a "state of excelling," more akin to having already attained, achieved, of being. "Better" are the incremental milestone improvements realized along the way on the path toward excellence.

In search of better should be a career-long commitment to elevate our professional job responsibilities, whatever they may be, to an art form. This quest is chronicled compellingly in *Jiro: Dreams of Sushi*. If you have yet to view this, it is well worth the time. It is the best $2.99 you will spend this year.

Some things to consider in your search of "better":

➢ Remember it is a personal journey. Compete with yourself and your potential. Never compare yourselves to others. What they do and accomplish is beyond your control and nothing more than a distraction.
➢ Needs to become a habit. It is about incremental improvement. Take an extended vacation from it, and you will fall behind. Strive to identify, uncover, or learn one work-related knowledge nugget each day. This adds up over weeks, months, and years.

➢ Is easier with mentors. They don't need to be in your company or even alive. If they happen to be above ground, reach out and engage them. You will be surprised at how receptive they will be to your questions.

➢ Requires discipline and resilience. Both will be your wingmen on your path to "better."

➢ Entails eliminating self-imposed limits. Eliminate them before they serve to eliminate you.

➢ Requires not trusting happiness. Circumstances change. A resolute commitment to "better" insulates you from the unexpected.

➢ Is understanding that small, incremental improvements will generate outsized returns. The best thing about sales is that you don't need to wait long to reap them.

➢ Is about the ABCs. Always Be Curious. Curiosity broadens your insight and perspective. Both are necessary to become "better."

➢ Requires practicing and rehearsing. "Better" is about learning new things, but it is also about making sure to retain mastery over what you've already learned.

➢ Is purposeful striving. "Better" is not an accident.

➢ Requires seeking out feedback, embracing it, and acting upon it, good or bad.

➢ Entails a few minutes of honest daily reflection.

➢ Welcomes the difficult. Easy won't make you better.

➢ Looks kindly upon the impatient. "Better" doesn't happen to those that wait.

➢ Recommends that we knock our commitment up a notch or two. It is okay to set aside some time on the weekend, morning, or evening for professional development, and this time need not come at the expense of family time.

➢ Is more readily attained by those who effectively manage their time (see immediately above).

➤ Contends that we try new stuff, experiment with our approach, and challenge our routine. Find out what works and what doesn't. Then either adopt or discard.
➤ Requires being uncomfortable with being comfortable.
➤ It has no finish line and that is the best part. The path to "better" has a beginning but no end.

These four words can serve to guide both our personal and professional lives. It is a thrilling, gratifying adventure that often leads to accomplishing what was initially thought to be unattainable.

Any company or team collectively searching in unison for "better" will soon find themselves in the midst of something extremely rare, special, and gratifying. Unlike the search for Sasquatch or the Loch Ness monster, the search for "better" will be much more fruitful. Why not begin the search today?

To: All Beasley Sales Managers
From: Bob McCurdy
9-8-19
RE: Blind Spots

Just noticed a big one in a car my wife just bought. I have to push the seat back so far to drive it that there is a dangerous blind spot to my left.

Blind spots. We all have them, and they are just as dangerous to our health when driving, as they are dangerous to our professional health and performance.

Like anything else that is dangerous, it is best to try to eliminate them or minimize them.

Do we have a blind spot for a particular salesperson due to longevity, rationalizing, or accepting their performance, production, or lack of digital productivity?

Do we have a blind spot for a particular advertiser? Extending to them a sweetheart deal they are no longer deserving of due to a personal relationship or historical precedent?

Do we have a blind spot for any internal systems that are in place that might have run their course?

Do we have a blind spot for any revenue opportunities that might be staring us in the face that we could take advantage of if we approached things a bit differently or viewed the landscape differently?

Do we have a blind spot regarding our current structure's effectiveness? Is there a better way to deploy our assets in light of the current revenue challenges and need for a breakout digital effort?

How about our own personal blind spots regarding ourselves and our performance? This is where feedback from our people and bosses can be beneficial. Even when we are aware of blind spots in others, we tend to discount them in ourselves. One study recently found that 85 percent of people surveyed believed they were less biased than the average person; only one person believed themselves to be more biased than average. Obviously not possible or true.

What is hiding in our blind spots?

To: All Beasley Sales Managers
From: Bob McCurdy
1-5-20
Re: Nothing

I asked my nine-year-old grandson the other day what he did over the holidays, and the response was, "Nothing."

It is impossible to do "nothing"—we are always doing "something," but "nothing" ever happens by doing "nothing." "Something" always happens when we do "nothing," and it is usually not good.

Doing "something" is preferable to doing "nothing." Actually, in most cases so is doing "anything," as it indicates some kind of action and at least we have the chance of stumbling upon our future or solving a problem.

Doing "nothing" is about maintaining the status quo. For every action there is a reaction, and doing "nothing" is a conscious choice of deferred action and is more often than not unpleasant. There is usually a hefty price paid for doing "nothing."

Made budgets are the sum total of a bunch of "somethings," a handful of "anythings," and infrequent "nothings."

What are the "somethings" we are doing differently in this fresh, new year? Cumulatively, they will determine our 12-31-20 YTD revenue.

Day-by-day excellence!

To: All Beasley Sales Managers
From: Bob McCurdy
1-26-20
Re: Our Best

I've often said, "I did my best." It might have been true, or, at times, it might have been a way to rationalize away a result.

A company's performance is the sum total of each employee's "best."

Is it our best, or is it our best as we traditionally defined it? Tradition can impede improvement.

Was it good enough? And even if was, is "good enough" enough?

If it wasn't, how do we make sure it is moving forward?

How does "our best" compare to our competitors? Should we care? Do we commoditize ourselves with such a comparison?

Is it in need of some rejuvenation/modification?

Does this year's version of "our best" differ from last year's?

Just as technology, fashion, and our taste in music continue to evolve, so must "our best."

To: All Beasley Sales Managers
From: Bob McCurdy
2-9-20
Re: Change lives

The other day my wife said to me, half-kidding, as I was leaving for the airport to visit one of our markets, "Go change some lives." I replied that it is kind of a difficult thing to do in one trip.

But she was absolutely correct; in the grander scheme that is exactly what successful leaders do—they change some lives.

We have a huge responsibility to our sales teams and clients to be the best leaders we can be, as what we say, do, and recommend impact them greatly. It is a responsibility and privilege we should never take lightly.

Leaders also change lives by creating other leaders—the next generation.

We are on our way to becoming a leader when we have our replacement on staff, or we have trained someone that has been promoted to another Beasley market.

Building a "bench" is a key responsibility of leaders. Ours could be deeper.

In sports, they often talk about a "coaching tree"—all of the assistant coaches that have once worked for a head coach who have moved on to become head coaches themselves. Those with the largest "trees" tend to be the best leaders, role models, and teachers.

We should all strive to be growing our own "coaching trees," seeding our teams and company with outstanding promotable talent and changing some lives in the process.

To: All Beasley Sales Managers
From: Bob McCurdy
2-23-20
Re: Your "Why"

"Why" is described as, "for what cause or purpose." Another word for cause is "mission" with "purpose" being the reason for the "mission." The Blues Brothers often said, "We're on a mission from God." Ours might not be as lofty, but it is important, nonetheless.

We all need a "why" beyond showing up every morning and putting in our ten and then heading home for dinner.

A "why" needs to be bigger than ourselves—noble and audacious—and will serve as our greatest source of energy and satisfaction throughout our careers.

"Why" needs to be bigger than simply making budget or keeping our jobs. If our mission and purpose are right things like hitting budget and remaining employed take care of themselves.

There are dozens of different "whys." Mine is simple, and it's the reason I walk to my desk every morning. It is to take everything I have learned in the past forty-four years and share/give it away to anyone who asks—to assist everyone and anyone who is interested in becoming more effective professionals.

What's yours?

To: All Beasley Sales Managers
From: Bob McCurdy
3-1-20
Re: Champions

A friend gave me the book *How Champions Think*. Some of what I highlighted follows. While there is not much new regarding this topic, there are different ways of saying the same thing about this subject:

➤ Competition teaches us about ourselves. It pushes us and pulls us to try things we might not try and change things we might not change in the absence of competition.

➤ While luck might affect outcomes, it does not affect effort.

➤ Go out there and create your own reality.

➤ In all too many corners of society, people are placing limits on themselves or accepting limits of others. When a person tells me that he is being "realistic," I hear a person putting limits on themselves.

➤ I can't control the competition, but I can control, my game, effort, and concentration.

➤ Bill Walsh's book *The Game Takes Care of Itself* expounds upon the importance of preparing meticulously and then let the chips fall where they may.

➤ There is no substitute for acquiring and polishing skills through practice. Remember, to become who you want to become means you must do what must be done, and that, like it or not, includes practice.

➤ They react to setbacks not by getting discouraged and giving up but with persistence. When Pat Riley and the Lakers lost to Houston in the NBA finals, he was asked how he felt. He replied, "Motivated."

➤ Given the choice between being single-minded and casual commitment, I'll take single-mindedness every time.

➤ There is a direct correlation between the work that goes "in" and the results that come "out."

➤ Most people have a lot more trouble with perseverance than with taking breaks.

Might be a few thoughts to share with your staffs.

CHAPTER 10

My Personal Philosophy— What I Believe Bone Deep

Live your belief and you can turn around the world.
—Henry David Thoreau,
American philosopher

What follows is something I sent four years ago to a salesperson who asked what attitudes and habits assisted me in my professional development. It epitomizes my philosophy:

At sixty-four, soon to be sixty-five, I have a handful of years to go, although I will probably never retire as there is still too much yet to accomplish and learn. After four decades in business, I feel as if I have just scratched the surface. I recall reading about a pianist named Vladimir Horowitz who was widely considered the best in the world. Horowitz practiced eight hours/day well into his eighties. I am not sure that is my endgame, but I have always felt if he could make that kind of commitment, so could I.

Commitment is about discipline, and the good thing about discipline is that it is within all of our control. There is enough in life and business that I can't control, so I like controlling what I can. The thing about sales success is that it does not require us to be Rhodes Scholars; it just requires that we have some degree of emotional intelligence, be somewhat pleasant, possess product expertise, be able to withstand rejection, and hustle. With hustle being the key characteristic.

In spite of possessing a decent amount of discipline, I have come nowhere near perfecting this business, which has always been my professional goal. Knowing I would not be able to perfect it was no reason not to pursue it. This might be sacrilegious for a sales exec to say, but money has never been my motivator. I have always believed that if I performed, continued to improve, and brought value to my company, the dollars and promotions would come. This belief has never let me down.

What has motivated me and continues to motivate me is the pursuit of excellence, becoming as good as one is capable of becoming—the narrowing of the gap between what I am currently accomplishing versus what I am capable of accomplishing. There is a purity in that pursuit that is good for the soul.

For me, it always boiled down to professional growth, getting better day by day, recognizing that a career is a decades-long marathon and not sprint. Attempting to narrow this "gap" requires effort, and effort was always something that has been within my control. I have liked that.

I have long felt that the greatest impediment to our success and professional growth is that our demands on ourselves are several notches below our capabilities. Stretching oneself to identify our "outer limits" is a noble endeavor. Stretch is about the difference between current performance and aspirations. The idea is not to just do enough to get by but to cheerfully chase excellence with vigor. Great salespeople typically expect more of themselves than their managers do, with the difference between accomplishing the "possible" and the "impossible" being their own determination. I have always liked that as well. I can control my own determination. Dare to achieve the impossible, and achieve the extraordinary. Funny thing about "impossible." It always is until it is not.

I read a quote some time ago that went something like, "The only things in life that you can truly keep are the things that you can give away" and many whom I've worked knew I would always do all within my power to make them successful, sharing whatever knowledge and expertise I've accrued. My goal now is to leave some "footprints" for the next generation to follow. Coach John Wooden of UCLA once said to me "that it's impossible to identify where a teacher's impact ends." To me that sounds like the ultimate footprint, so here is my shot at leaving a few that will assist you on your path to success:

The first step toward excellence is deciding that you in fact want to be excellent and understanding that it does not require perfection. Excellence is not something that happens by accident. It does not just "occur." No one has ever "wished" or "sat" their way to excellence. It has to be pursued, is never easy, and often elusive. It requires tremendous discipline, which could be the most important "skill" for anyone who is pursuing excellence. Little of value can be accomplished without discipline. With it, anything can. You can refine and enhance your discipline. It is within your control.

Now that you decided you want to become special, the next step is to identify what exactly you are willing to give up. It takes practice, study, hard work, which must come at the expense of other activities you might rather be doing like napping, hanging around, relaxing, partying. Once you have decided what you are going to "give up," you need to cultivate and nurture the self-discipline to continue on this path. This often requires an "act of will," which requires you to overcome yourself in some fashion or revert to your old ways. This can be accomplished by committing to what Gandhi called a "singleness of decision." You tell yourself you are going to do something, and every time you begin to feel like you do not want to do it, you remind yourself that you committed to yourself that you would do it.

Never compare yourself to others. You have no control over

them. When you do this, you commoditize yourself. Making comparisons hurts you so much more than it helps. You are unique with unique skills and goals. The fact that someone else is doing something or not doing something is irrelevant to your success and your future. Just focus on piloting your life. The definition of success and excellence of the individuals to whom you are comparing yourself might be far different from yours. Avoid the crowd. The person who follows the crowd will likely go no further than the crowd. The individual who walks alone will likely find his or her self where no one has been before.

Develop a challenging daily routine and stick to it. Exception weakens the habit. This routine needs to be inviolate. It must become what you do and the essence of who you are professionally. Your daily routine becomes your ritual and road map to success when things get difficult.

Understand that excellence is a long, trying process. You have to "be" before you can "do"; you have to "do" before you can "have." You just can't snap your fingers and suddenly be outstanding. Great performers are in a perpetual state of "becoming" so that you can "be," "do" and ultimately "have." "Becoming" requires discipline, effort, and commitment, all of which motivates great performers and, again, is within your control.

Great performers constantly challenge their assumptions regarding what is "possible," often asking themselves, "Why not?" Peak performers are always redefining "what should be," preparing themselves for what "will be," while respecting what "has been" but not held prisoner by it.

One of the greatest principles of success in the entire world is the belief in persistence—the attitude that "If I persist long enough, I will win." It is the willingness to suffer, sacrifice, and work harder than the next person. Hard work does not guarantee success, but it is virtually impossible to succeed without it. Your own determination to succeed is the single most important ingredient to your success.

Inertia is the #1 enemy of excellence. Smack it down. Genius is not in the size of our actions, but in the relentlessness of them. The one who quits last usually wins, as failure always follows the path of least persistence.

There is no financial investment that will generate a greater return than investing in your own professional development. The fact that your company is not going to pick up an expense should never deter us from incurring that expense. If it makes you better and enables you to deliver greater value to your clients and if it makes you a more effective, more knowledgeable professional, do not hesitate to pay for it out of pocket. There is no greater investment than investing in yourself. It will come back to you hundredfold.

Voraciously pursue knowledge by becoming a lifelong student of your profession. Make a commitment to not put your head on your pillow at night until you have learned something that day that you can utilize professionally the rest of your career. Your knowledge and expertise are your professional "currency," the reason why your clients rely on you and not the competition. You must pursue this knowledge and expertise relentlessly. When it comes to learning and refining your skills, there is no top of the mountain, there is no final destination; you never "arrive," you just need to keep climbing. Most would agree knowledge is power, but most also fail to do something about it. Your goal should be towering competence, which cannot be attained without towering knowledge. What distinguishes a good surgeon from a great one is knowledge. It is the same in sales.

Always strive to be better on Monday than you were on Friday. Remember Monday-Friday is for keeping up with the competition. The weekends are for getting ahead of them. The beautiful thing about sales is that you can immediately utilize on Monday what you have learned on Saturday and Sunday.

Great salespeople treat each day as if it is their first day on the job. Do not allow your zest and enthusiasm for this business to atrophy. I have noticed at times that the more successful some sellers became, the more they liked hard work less, and they began to work less hard. Inoculate yourself from this FWMTS disease—"Forgot what made them successful." Success is often fleeting enough. A little insecurity keeps you hungry and sharp. The way to be professionally "safe" is to avoid being professionally "secure."

"Good enough" is the enemy of the "great"; practice constructive dissatisfaction. Always be looking for ways to make the "good" "great"—including yourself. When you do all that is required "and then some," you will usually win. Never allow "good enough" to be good enough. You are what you repeatedly do.

Understand that "you" make "you." Never wait for someone else to teach or train you. It is great when they do, but do not wait. It is also critical that you have an absolute and total belief that what you are selling is worth more than what you are asking. Professional expertise is one of the great ways of generating this belief and separating ourselves from the competition.

Too many people in business have forgotten that just as much, if not more, study is required once you graduate from college and become paid professionals in the sales field. Perpetual professional curiosity pays huge dividends.

Make no mistake about it, you make the account list, not vice versa. The excellent salespeople understand that they are their company's true competitive advantage. Peddlers take the rate their clients give them. Sales professionals get the rate and share their stations deserve. If you are in management, it is your job to make sure the peddlers work for the competition.

Identify ways to establish points of distinction. Many salespeople have lost their own points of distinction because they do nothing more than the minimum. Go out of your way to identify ways of delivering heroic service—service so good your client brags about it. "Ordinary" sucks. A product sold in an "ordinary" way by an "ordinary" salesperson will develop an "ordinary" image and generate "ordinary" revenue and nothing more.

The amount of value added that you generate for your company is the difference between the revenue you generate versus what your competitors would generate if both products were equally desirable. The excellent seller understands this and continually strives to widen this gap.

Excellent salespeople rarely peg their ability to get an order based on price. They SOQNOP—sell on quality and not on price. Great salespeople recognize that they are their company's biggest competitive advantage and sell accordingly. They don't let all the reasons "why not" get in the way of getting things done.

One of life's greatest joys is the purity of striving to live up to your own potential. Everyone gets the same 1,440 minutes each day to make choices, pursue opportunities, and strive for excellence. These 1,440 minutes cannot be exchanged, replaced, or refunded, and there's only one per person, per day. The excellent salesperson constantly asks throughout the day whether what they are currently doing is going to make them better. If the answer is "no" they immediately switch gears. You are the sum of the choices you make. If you are not where you want to be in your career, you are the result of your compromises. The good thing is there is still time to accomplish what you want to accomplish.

I will leave you with this one question: What will you do today to elevate yourselves and your job performance to a completely new level in your pursuit of excellence? There is little I can "guarantee," but one thing I can guarantee is that your commitment to this pursuit of excellence will inspire both your clients and your coworkers. Most importantly though, it will inspire you. Choose excellence and become professionally significant!

CHAPTER 11

My Leadership "47"

A boss has the title; a leader has the people.
—Simon Sinek,
author

What follows are my forty-seven tenets to becoming a leader of consequence. Effective leaders:

1. Understand there is not one style of great leadership, but there are inviolate traits that contribute to great leadership—honesty, emotional intelligence, empathy, integrity, hard work, role model worthiness, and trustworthiness. Effective leadership boils down to traits and not personality.
2. Thank and acknowledge employees for a job well done, understanding the importance of recognizing extraordinary efforts and performance.
3. Clear out the "underbrush." Eliminating all the impediments that contribute to underperformance and create the conditions for success for their teams. They clear the runways so the salespeople can flourish. Leaders often ask, "What challenges are you facing; where are you stuck?" and then do something about it.

4. Appreciate the fact that leaders are "made," not born. Leadership is learned just as any other skill can be learned. So many people want an "e=mc2" formula for leadership. It does not exist. There are not any shortcuts. Leadership is hard work, and most of it is on-the-job training. Effective leadership is not a straight line up; there are many twists and turns that need to be experienced before leadership excellence is attained, and once attained, it must continue to be nurtured and built upon.

5. Know that they are only as valid as the output of the people around them.

6. Embrace that the sign of a good leader is not how many followers they have but how many leaders they create. Effective leaders simply create more leaders. You can tell how effective someone has been as a leader by how many other leaders are in his/her leadership "tree."

7. Have relentlessly high standards, continually raising the bar.

8. Don't operate under a traditional pyramidal structure but in an inverted pyramid instead. Leaders work for their people, making it easier for their team to do their jobs. Leaders are their water boys and water girls, doing whatever it is they can to enhance the productivity of their teams.

9. Possess the guts to make unpopular decisions in defense of excellence, their vision, and their expectations, understanding that exceptions, however few, can easily undermine their leadership.

10. Understand that it is better to be respected for the right reasons than liked for the wrong ones.

11. Must be comfortable inducing a certain amount of positive tension, challenging team members to extend themselves beyond their current "selves."

Below is from Dom Milano, who started at Katz in our research department and rose to salesperson, sales manager to Divisional VP, and has had an extremely successful post-Katz career.

> While watching the Last Dance recently, I was reminded of my fourteen-plus years at Katz Radio. While the Bulls were dominating on the court in the '90s, Katz was dominating the radio rep world. Katz Radio. The Best. These were not just words on paper. They were part of the culture and the mindset, both of which were led by Bob McCurdy. An injury prevented Bob, legitimately a great college basketball player, from playing his own game in the NBA. However, just as Jordan did with the Bulls, Bob brought his intensity to the radio business and Katz.
>
> Like Mike, Bob demanded "The Best." Bob created "positive tension" and sometimes it wasn't easy to deal with. However, as I and so many others, managed our way through it, there was a realization. You become The Best by not accepting anything but being The Best. You do "whatever it takes" and anything less is unacceptable. You don't develop mental toughness and fortitude in a lax environment. Jordan wouldn't have had 6 championships without it, and Katz would never have dominated the way it did without McCurdy.
>
> Bob was tough but those of us who had the benefit of working for him always knew he cared—about us as individuals and about leading an organization to greatness. It was that combination of care and

high expectations that allowed us to appreciate the environment Bob created. The truth is that there are so many people in the radio and audio business today who were positively impacted by Bob's influence. Their success and mine is a testament to the culture and leadership Bob provided us.

Dom Milano
SVP/Sales and Business Development
Targetspot

12. Great leaders can get their people to pull from themselves things they didn't know were there.
13. Must sustain unremitting focus on the professional standards of their staff, to establish a level of performance below which the individual and team refuses to go. Expectations define the leader and team. If the leaders refuse anything but the best, they usually get it.
14. Should never manage by nostalgia. As General Electric's Jack Welsh once said, "You got to look reality in the eye and then act upon it." To do otherwise is to manage by hope and is leadership malpractice.
15. There is no managerial skill getting "good" performance from "good" people. Excellent leaders consistently get "great" performance from "good" people and good performance from those with average skills.
16. Don't accept excuses. Effective leaders can get their people to look within themselves when things don't go according to plan and limit the use of the pointed finger.
17. Induce "stretch." The mediocre leader is not conscious of the discrepancy between what they are requiring of their staff versus what they are capable of accomplishing,

mistakenly believing they are operating at the outer limits of their potential but are far from it.

18. Possess what the Tin Man, the Lion, and Scarecrow were searching for in *The Wizard of Oz*—a brain, a heart, and courage. Effective leaders also need a funny bone, a wishbone, and backbone.

19. Understand that no personnel turnover can be a problem if performance standards are to continually progress upward. I refer to this as "managerial-generated turnover." It is simply not possible for a company or team to reach its potential with C and D players. If they are not capable of becoming As or Bs, they need to be replaced.

20. Recognize that companies are great when the quality of the personnel is high from top to bottom, not when there is just a handful of super overachievers. This requires the staff being consistently upgraded the same way general managers of sports teams try to upgrade their teams. Effective leaders understand that great people do not guarantee success, but no company can become great without great people. They are constantly on the lookout for exceptional talent who can challenge the existing staff to raise their games.

21. Must also learn the fine art of followership. Good leaders are the kind of followers they expect their people to be.

22. Are learners, understanding that when their learning is finished, their impact as a leader is finished. Strong leaders model this learning mentality for all to see, understanding that they must master themselves before they can expect others to do the same. Part of this process is continued learning. Leaders frequently ask themselves what attitudes, behaviors, or habits they need to modify and what specific actions they should take to improve themselves before they attempt to improve others. Effective leaders are indefatigable in search of "better."

23. Go to extremes in matters of principle. Integrity is not a sometimes thing. Either you have it, or you do not. The best definition I have heard for integrity is that it is the fundamental value leaders place on themselves. Leaders with integrity spend the better part of their careers establishing their reputation and communicating their character, which is why they treat integrity as an inviolate habit and extend it to all aspects of their life.

24. Must be visionaries. There are no mature industries only tired imaginations.

25. Possess empathy. They can take the same set of facts and shift their vantage point to view the situation through a different lens. Respecting, not necessarily adopting, different points of view.

26. Relentlessly search for ways to communicate their key, core expectations in new and different ways via stories, examples, and analogies to keep the message fresh. Great leaders can make old things new.

27. Are A students of history. They learn from the past but remain focused on the present with a keen eye on the future, recognizing that the future is where they and their teams are going to be spending the rest of their careers. They are always on the lookout for competitive threats.

28. Understand leadership does not imply rigidity. They master the flexibility dance. Great leaders understand that no matter how thin the pancake, there are always two sides to everything.

29. Recognize they will make mistakes, quickly admit them, and when necessary apologize for them. They understand that an admission of error is an expression of strength and use this fact to their advantage. What follows is a recent email I received from an individual who used to work for me. I had forgotten this incident, but he sure did not:

Howdy! Congrats on your retirement!!! I want to say that I only had the honor of working for you for five years but, I loved it! No one more mentoring, harder working (although you could've gotten to the office a bit earlier 😄) or more fair. You always backed us up when we were right and kicked our asses when we were wrong. I'll never forget one day you really blasted me. I couldn't tell you what about, if you put a gun to my head but, what I know is that you came back in to my office about 15 minutes later, apologized and we talked it through. You will always be the gold standard for me. I have a note on my desk of something you once told me: "Create your own wind!" I also have your file of quotes! Again, a privilege to have been able to work with you. Warmest regards, CK

30. Are excellent listeners seeking to understand exactly what the individual to whom he/she is speaking is saying and are mindful responders choosing their words carefully, understanding the weight they carry with those being lead.
31. Exude optimism. A leader's optimism is contagious. Excellent leaders encourage followers to believe they are superior to their challenges, which motivates the entire team to achieve goals and be at their best.
32. Must be "causationists." Appreciating the fact that they are being compensated to make things happen and achieve company goals. They understand their legacy will be based upon what they did or did not do and readily accept this fact.
33. Great leaders never pass up the opportunity to teach.
34. Understand the speed of the leader determines the pace of the pack. Every company moves at the pace of its leadership.

If the leader sits back and relaxes, members of their teams will sit back and relax. If the leader compromises, the entire organization compromises.

35. Appreciate that their life is their message. It is impossible to maximize their effectiveness as a leader if their personal lives are a mess. The best leaders are well-rounded role models who balance both life and business. John Wooden once said the two most important words in the English language were "love" and "balance." "Balance" is a key contributor to a leader's success, and setting a good example is the best "sermon."

36. Embrace the fact that managers produce order, leaders produce change and commitment. All managers are not effective leaders.

37. Understand that you can lead people more effectively by inspiring than by facts and reason.

38. Recognize that what is as valuable to a leader as ability is the ability to recognize ability.

39. Appreciate that their people's needs must come first. Great leaders remain trustworthy even in times of great stress and will always put the needs of their team and organization ahead of their own. Leaders serve their people, and this service is based upon values that will not be compromised when circumstances deteriorate.

40. Set aside time for reflection, which is just an honest "conversation" with themselves. It is a good way to double-check their decisions and retain professional balance.

41. Are like orchestra conductors. What a great conductor achieves is the belief in great violinists and cellists that they are taking part in something that only the conductor can provide. The effective leader can do the same, convincing their teams that they are taking part in creating something significant that only the leader can deliver. This leads to

outstanding performance and contributes to minimizing A performer turnover.

42. Get dirty, standing in the mud and trenches with their people, learning their team's work, putting their skin in the game every day, get their team's problems solved, and stay with them until they are resolved. They do not lead from behind; they get actively involved and lead, putting their reputation on the line to work hand-in-hand with their people to accomplish challenging goals. This type of leadership involvement is necessary for great morale, loyalty, and outstanding performance.

43. Are not the same leader this week that they were last week; they are better. Great leaders are constantly evolving, not allowing themselves to become complacent or grow old in their jobs.

44. Judge people based on their strengths. There was a book years ago, *Soar with Your Strengths*, which suggested focusing on people's strengths. Let rabbits run not climb, squirrels climb not swim, and fish swim and not fly. Manage to people's strengths not weaknesses.

45. Don't avoid difficult conversations. Leaders owe it to their teams to have these conversations. Everyone wants to know "where they stand," and the best way to accomplish this is to be honest and not avoid having the difficult discussion.

46. Are careful not to overly identify with their teams. Overly identifying with them can lead to accepting excuses and reasons for underperformance. Effective leaders are careful to maintain some "distance" between themselves and those they lead.

47. Needs a sense of humor and to be able to laugh, even at times at themselves. I'll let Mike Agovino tell a story:

While Bob was a taskmaster with great discipline, he did have a sense of humor and was able to laugh at himself.

When I was GSM at Katz Radio and Bob was President we starting having prospective sales people take "personality profile" tests that aimed to match their skills and characteristics to an ideal candidate profile we had created. After three consecutive prospects performed badly on the test, I complained to Bob that I thought it was not always accurate. He told me the system was solid and he was going to take a test himself just to prove it.

I had a feeling he would follow through on his threat quickly so I told his assistant to let me know if he did. Sure enough, the next day Bob took it but submitted it using an alias. His assistant gave me the alias so I was able to flag it with the folks that processed the tests and while Bob's alias had scored very well, the actual report would not find its way to Bob. Instead, with the help of a few coconspirators we were able to doctor a report that gave Bob the worst score we had ever seen on the test. Bob had no idea he'd been duped when he reviewed the results.

After reviewing his atrocious results, he called me into his office and told me that he now thought these tests "sucked." It was all I could do to not burst into laughter.

After that, Bob let me hire a prospect or two that did not do so well on the test if I believed strongly the candidate was the right one. He complimented me on my creative problem solving.

While we worked it hard at Katz, we knew how to have fun too. Bob took his responsibilities very seriously, but he didn't take himself too seriously. I think this aspect of his personality contributed significantly to his ability to lead. This is one but one of at least a dozen others we pulled on Bob over the years. He was always a good sport and laughed as hard as we did.

CHAPTER 12

Does This Stuff Work?

The stuff that works best is driven
by passion rather than dollars.

—Craig Newmark,
Craigslist founder

I still remember shortly before my dad passed, we were sitting in his kitchen when he said, "God must surely be looking down at you." I asked, "Why, Dad?" and he replied, "I still can't believe you made a living in sales." I replied, "I guess a little focus, discipline, and effort goes a long way." He would have been pleasantly surprised, and I believe proud, had he had the opportunity to read emails like those that follow.

So, is the wisdom in this book worthy of consideration? No doubt about it. It just needs to be embraced and "lived."

Jamie Kriegel/SVP, Nat'l Spot and Digital Underwriting at NPR
From: Jamie Kriegel <JKriegel@npr.org>
Sent: Monday, April 13, 2020 2:24 PM

To: Bob McCurdy <bob.mccurdy@bbgi.com>
Subject: Thank You

Bob—I read your announcement and it's hard to envision a radio world without you on active duty. Thank you for the incredible impact you have had on my career and—as crazy as this sounds—most of my adult life. The career part is easy. I am one of a long list of radio professionals who have had the distinct honor of being trained and developed by THE BEST. From Repordy to adlets to "knowing your numbers" to preparing candidates for "The Bob McCurdy Interview" and everything in between, you've instilled in me a commitment to "BE GREAT." Knowing I had to be sharp at any moment when the words "I have Bob McCurdy for you" are shouted across the office has made me a better professional.

Post-Katz, you have always been there when I've had a question or needed your POV. It never mattered what hat was worn, if there was an opportunity to make someone better, you would not hesitate. Posted on my office wall to this day is your "Stand out from the Sales Crowd" article in Radio Ink. 50% of the reason its posted is to serve as a reminder of what it takes to separate from the rest of the pack. The other 50% is the image of your face strategically placed directly above my phone. "If Bob was standing next to you, how would he say you sounded" is the litmus test I give with every call.

The impact you will always have on my life is deeper. Foremost, what you have taught me extends well beyond the sales desk and I often find myself implementing your teachings with my children. Second, I have made dozens of lifelong friends from this industry with our one common denominator being that we were all hired and/ or trained by you. My family of five have grown together and enjoy a blessed life in Los Angeles thanks in large part to you transferring me out here over twenty years ago when my wife and I were building our foundation. Speaking of LA, I felt so honored to join you on a couple occasions with the "Wizard of Westwood." Those memories will last forever.

Bob, over the twenty-five-plus years we've known each other (can you believe it?), I've learned more from you than any other person on the planet with the exception of my father. I cherish our friendship and hope you are cool if I continue to seek your wisdom. Here's wishing you the very best as you transition to retirement, BEAT cancer, and enjoy you some YOU time. You have an army of people in your corner.

Please stay in touch and I will do the same. BE GREAT—Jaybo.

<u>Jill Albert/ President and Founder of Direct Results Marketing</u>
From: Jill Albert <jill@directresults.com>
Sent: Saturday, April 11, 2020 10:55 AM
To: Bob McCurdy <bob.mccurdy@bbgi.com>
Subject: Re: JA, i have retired ... was time to

Congratulations!

You are the strongest and most influential voice this industry has known. The knowledge you have shared has driven a myriad of ideas and an infinite number of new campaigns. Your leadership and example has set the bar for many thousands and will continue to influence generations to come. Your honesty, enthusiasm and commitment has relaunched my love and pure passion for this business.

I am beyond thrilled to know you and so grateful for your help and the influence you have shared with our team. I can't imagine how many careers, campaign, PEOPLE you alone have made BETTER ... let's take a wild guess how many have learned from Bob McCurdy ...?!

Just about every day I reference my Bob McCurdy archives. Every Saturday morning we look forward to the lessons you share, the perspective that lifts our minds and spirits and make pure sense when we are challenged, or on top of the world or questioning everything.

Today I simply say THANK YOU and WOW. You are truly AMAZING and beyond INSPIRATIONAL. It is an honor and a celebration to know you. You are a beacon.

Take care, get better, read, play, enjoy!

Looking forward to seeing you as soon as possible. Thank You—Thank You—THANK YOU!

Jeff Howard/ President of National Sales at IHeartMedia:

Saw the news. 45 years. You are the John Wooden of Radio Bob. Thank you for all you have done for so many. We can count on one hand over the decades the real leaders that have displayed your level of courage in and out of the business. You are on the Mount Rushmore of our space.

Melanie Morris/ Account Director, Client Solutions at Nielsen Audio:

From: Melanie Morris
Sent: Sunday, April 12, 2020 3:55 PM
To: Bob McCurdy <bob.mccurdy@bbgi.com>
Subject: Your Retirement

Bob you are such an enormous influence in my life. My brief post didn't do justice. You gave me the chance many others did not. My time at Katz taught me many of life's most valuable lessons—whether in parenting, personal relationships, professional relationships, with oneself … all in the pursuit of excellence. You've made me feel honored to be a member of an elite team. I hadn't a clue what I was getting myself into when we met. Truly, I could've been talking to McGavern or the like. I didn't know what I didn't know. I revere you just the same as I feared you. I love invoking your name—if people don't already know it, the hidden message is that's their deficiency. Please be well and joyful. Melanie

Tony Pino/VP Sales/National Sales at iHeartMedia:
From: Pino, Tony <TonyPino@iheartmedia.com>
Sent: Thursday, April 16, 2020 2:05 PM
To: Bob McCurdy <bob.mccurdy@bbgi.com>
Subject: Hello Bob and Thank You!

Hello Bob,

We haven't spoken in a few years and I just read in the trades this week that you have "officially" retired from the business. Congratulations and thank you for everything that you have provided to this business.

I've been sitting here thinking about what to write in this email to express how genuinely appreciative I am for all that you taught me and I've concluded that no amount of words would do the trick. You accepted me into this business and were my first mentor in Radio. I've been lucky enough to be in this business for close to seventeen years and have had a front row seat to watch it grow and cultivate to what it has become today. No matter how much it changes, every now and then I look back at an email you sent me in 2008 that included some of your "truisms." The art of Sales will never change and these "truisms" will always stand the test of time!

- *the very first step to succeeding at a job is to become genuinely interested in it.*
- *become a student of your profession, life and people.*
- *the mediocre seller tells, the good one explains and the great one inspires*
- *integrity is not a "sometimes" thing.*
- *practice, drill and rehearse.*
- *Mark Twain said it takes two weeks to prepare for an impromptu speech*

Thank you, Mr. McCurdy from the bottom of my heart and wishing you a happy and healthy retirement!

PS … don't worry my pitch book is still up to date ☺

Mark Stewart/ Ex EVP Chief Strategy Officer/Townsquare Media, ex VP Global Brand Services Kraft Foods:
Sent: Wednesday, April 15, 2020 1:58 PM
To: Bob McCurdy <bob.mccurdy@bbgi.com>
Subject: Congratulations

Read in *Radio News* that you are hanging up your spurs. Well-done, well-deserved and well-played sir.

You are an icon, a gentleman and a trusted leader in our industry. Your commitment and contributions to the betterment of radio are immeasurable and you have been a voice of reason, inspiration, consistency and credibility to the expanded community—radio, research, agencies and brands.

Would love to stay in touch, as our conversations have always been intelligent, inspiring and insightful.

So, there you go, I include these emails not to blow my own horn but to provide additional substantiation that what appears in the previous pages works! Hell, when I got out of college no one wanted to hire me, and I was a well-known name. That is how bad I was. This stuff can make a difference.

I remember when I first got to New York to manage the office, a seller whom I respected said to me, "I came quietly, and I will leave quietly." I have tried to do the same. It has been a long and winding road. I was diagnosed with rectal cancer at the beginning of 2018, given radiation and chemotherapy in May-June of '18 only to find out in December of 2018 that the hospital had given me the incorrect dosage of chemotherapy, only 25 percent of the prescribed amount. Not what any patient wants to hear. It has been quite a ride with an uncertain ending, which has a way of putting things into perspective. Throughout this ordeal, I have constantly reminded myself to take the advice I would have given someone else in a similar situation.

We all have a choice of how we live and how we depart. Both should be done with dignity and integrity. The lessons I have discussed have helped me immeasurably throughout this ordeal.

The Rolling Stones in their song "Time Waits for No One," sang, "Hours are like diamonds, don't let them waste." I used to listen to that song just before I walked out of my Richmond dorm room to head to the Robins Center to play a game to remind myself to give it my best shot, that there weren't too many games remaining, and not look back and say woulda, shoulda, coulda. The lyrics have a little different meaning now.

It is my hope that whatever your professional goals, you were able to walk away with some insights and helpful observations that will come in handy in your own quest for excellence.

Added Value

Not long ago, one of our research analysts at Katz, Don Jones, who worked at Katz years ago, posted on Facebook a reference to the three booklets I wrote in the 1990s: "Epic reads. Still resonate today. Thank you, Bob McCurdy, for fundamental sales and life lessons."

It seems like these booklets just might have stood the test of time. I listed the contents of two of them on the following pages. Each is as originally written.

Volume 1: Everything We Taught You in the Katz Training Program Paraphrased

Sales Calls

➤ Client calls: Be prepared, buttoned up, and don't waste their time. Our clients are busy attempting to run a business. Respect this fact.

➤ Nothing takes the place of "being there." The absent are always wrong. Don't "be" absent—"be" there.

➤ Know where you stand with your clients. Be honest with yourself. Concentrate on improving relationships where you are most vulnerable. Relationships count—a lot! People don't buy from people they don't like.

Attitude

➤ The best salespeople approach each day as if it were their first day on the job.

➢ The way to be professionally "safe" is never be professionally "secure." Do not stop doing things that made you successful in the first place. Avoid the FWMTS trap.

➢ The more successful people become, the more they like hard work less, and then they begin to work less hard. Inoculate yourself from this phenomenon. Success is fleeting if not properly nurtured. The secret is in the daily rigor.

➢ Avoid taking the path of least resistance. Resist shortcuts. Do what you know should be done when it needs to be done. We typically know the right thing to do; the hard part is consistently doing it.

➢ If you are ever unsure about a situation, follow your heart and be honest. Too much time is wasted thinking up excuses. Have fun, work hard, and be truthful. People respect that. Lincoln once said, "No man has a good enough memory to be a successful liar." He was not wrong.

➢ Advantage comes not from the spectacular but from the persistent seeking of the mundane edge. Execute the fundamentals every day—it provides you with a major competitive advantage.

➢ To be successful, your clients must enjoy doing business with you. Enthusiasm, excitement, conviction, and energy lead to better and deeper relationships and success.

➢ Strong convictions precede great actions. The way to develop strong convictions is through knowledge. Great performance will soon follow. Knowledge leads to conviction, conviction leads to confidence, confidence leads to effectiveness, and effectiveness leads to revenue.

➢ Have patience. Most things are difficult before they become easy. Repetition erases difficulty. It is not that difficult tasks are getting easier; you are just getting better at doing them.

➤ We are what we repeatedly do. Take the shortcut and you will have a short career. There are no shortcuts to anyplace worth going.

➤ Rising to meet the challenge is a trait of the successful seller. The love of a good fight. A great salesperson thrives on the challenge and the competition.

➤ Every job you do is a self-portrait. Autograph it with quality.

➤ "Good enough" is the worst enemy of "the best." "Good enough" might be acceptable at other companies but not here. Strive for excellence. Good enough is never good enough.

➤ A winner knows how much more they need to learn even when considered experts by others. Excellence is never having learned enough. It is the constant desire to master your profession.

➤ Selling without emotion is like a soft drink without carbonation or peanuts without salt. Say it with conviction, and you will convince.

➤ Compete relentlessly. There is no other way to succeed.

Effort

➤ Success is largely about hanging on when others have let go. Persevere. Sometimes we achieve our greatest successes when we don't have enough sense to quit.

➤ You don't learn to drive a car by watching. Force yourself to do things that make you uncomfortable. It will make you better.

➤ Achievement comes after hard work, not before. No successful salesperson ever sat their way to the top. Work it.

➤ There is an inexorable link between sustained effort and coming out on top.

Hustle

➢ There is no genius in life like the genius of perseverance. If you want something, work for it and nurture the will to accomplish it.

➢ Everyone knows what they want, but few know what they are willing to give up to get it. Know what you are willing to give up to achieve your goals.

➢ Sometimes, the order goes to the salesperson who waits, but they are usually only orders passed up by those who hustled. Hustle covers up mistakes and lack of experience.

➢ There are three kinds of workers. Those that "watch" things happen, those that "wondered" what happened, and those that "make" it happen. Be the latter.

➢ There is nothing easier than being busy and nothing harder than being productive. Know the difference. Ants are busy but not always productive.

➢ Half efforts don't cut it. If it is worth doing, do it with all your heart. You don't jump a ditch half at a time.

➢ Friday afternoons are a perfect time to work it hard. It tends to be less hectic at our clients' and agencies' place of business, and the competition is winding down for the weekend. Work Friday afternoons the same way you work Tuesday afternoons. If we wasted money the way we often waste time on Fridays, we would all be bankrupt.

Improvement

➢ Continually look for new ways to improve. Network. There are dozens of ways to make ourselves more effective. Many blunder in business through the inability or unwillingness to accept new ideas and stretch themselves, to become the engine of their own self-improvement. He/she who stops getting better stops being good. Keep your eyes open and your antennae up. You can learn from everyone with whom you come in contact.

➤ If it is not perfect, try to make it better. Constructive dissatisfaction is a key component to success.

Integrity

➤ Your reputation is your most important asset. Never do anything that could harm it. No sale is important enough to put your reputation at risk. The best way to manage your reputation is to do the right thing every time, every day.

Knowledge

➤ To be successful in business and to enhance your skills you need to study as much as you did in school, if not more. Those that move up the ladder of success have a firmer grasp of the nuances of their business. This doesn't happen without study.

➤ You must have absolute and total belief that what you are selling is worth more than what you are asking. To get to this point you must know your product and its benefits inside out.

➤ You can't become great unless you are up on the happenings in your industry. Stay current even if it means dipping into your pocket and subscribing to certain publications or attending conventions on your own dime.

Listen

➤ Listen intently. They are telling you how to sell them.

➢ Listening is the only way to identify USOs (unidentified sales objections). It is impossible to learn while talking. Know when to be quiet.

➢ You have two ears and one mouth for a reason. If you don't hear what people need, you will never sell them. Listen with respect.

Office

➢ Your personal office or your desk is a reflection of you. Keep it neat and professional in appearance. If you see something on the floor, pick it up. The same goes for the restrooms. If we saw something on the floor in our home, we would pick it up. We should do the same at the office.

➢ The more organized you are, the more successful you will be. It is that simple.

Prepare

➢ You never get a second chance for a first impression. You are being evaluated the minute you meet someone. Be prepared, be prompt, and be professional.

➢ Everyone wants to succeed, but few are willing to prepare to succeed. Success is 90 percent preparation and 10 percent presentation. Mark Twain was right when he said, "It takes two weeks to prepare for an impromptu speech."

➢ Vladimir Horowitz, considered the greatest pianist in the world, practiced eight hours/day well into his eighties. If he can do it, all of us in our twenties, thirties, and forties can certainly practice, drill, and rehearse our skills. It is on the weekends that we pull ahead of the pack.

> ➤ Thinking is the hardest work there is, which is why so few people do it. Think before you talk and act.
> ➤ Success is luck; just ask any "failure." Luck happens when preparation meets opportunity. Always be ready for your opportunity to shine and sell.

Sales

> ➤ It is very simple; do what you say you are going to do when you say you are going to do it. You will set yourself apart.
> ➤ Compartmentalize. Don't let something that happened in the morning negatively impact your performance in the afternoon. Remain fully focused on the task at hand. Always be in the present. Let the disappointments *go*!
> ➤ You will make mistakes. You will blow a sale; you will not believe some of the things you have said or did. We have all been there, but we must learn from our mistakes, taking great care not to repeat them. Remember failure is an opportunity to begin more intelligently. Critique yourself. Understand what went wrong and why, then proceed forward but never forget. The only way to avoid making mistakes is to have no ideas. We want you to have ideas and keep trying.
> ➤ People don't care how much you know until they know how much you care. Show all with whom you deal how much you care—every day. The best way to succeed in business is to put the client's interest first. When they succeed, you succeed.
> ➤ Ask and you will receive. Always ask for the business. You will write more business if you do.
> ➤ It is the little things done consistently that make the big things happen. All the key sales fundamentals are so simple, yet so few people consistently execute them.

There is genius in the small stuff just as small things—if not corrected—always become big things, *always*. Little mistakes join forces to become big mistakes. Is there a gap between how we are doing our jobs and the way we know we should do our jobs? If so, narrow it.

➤ You know you are getting better when your clients and management use these adjectives to describe you to someone: consistent, curious, energetic, focused, genuine, informative, inventive, knowledgeable, polished, respectful, responsive, sincere, timely, valuable.

➤ Salesmanship consists of transferring your conviction to a prospect, so before a salesperson can sell anything, they must sell themselves on the product, which means understanding its USPs.

➤ There is a difference between "interest" and "commitment." Let our competition be interested. We are committed. They like the business. We love it. Your commitment and conviction will inspire both your clients and your coworkers, but most importantly, it will inspire you. Knowledge leads to conviction, which leads to passion. Passion equals energy. You must share that passion/energy every opportunity. Our clients and buyers need to read it in our eyes.

➤ Learning is analogous to eating. You never graduate from eating, and we should never graduate from learning. Be sponge-like when it comes to learning more about your trade.

➤ Master the "bilities": responsibility, accountability, dependability, adaptability, credibility, compatibility, availability, stability, capability, and sustainability, dependability, reliability, and accountability. Be someone everyone can count on and one who continually delivers.

> ➤ Know the competition. Their strengths, their weakness, where they have relationships. We don't compete in a vacuum. It will help guide what and how we present.
> ➤ Remember to keep things in perspective. There is such a thing as being too serious. For maximum success, take your responsibilities but not yourselves too seriously.
> ➤ If we lose a piece of business, look inward. Ultimately, if something isn't sold, it is on us and no one else. Put your energies to positive use by focusing on how you will get it sold next time.
> ➤ Employ both logic and emotion when selling for maximum effectiveness. Logic gets them thinking and emotion gets them to act. Rely only on logic, and you will have the best-educated prospects and few sales. Rely only on emotion, and you will have a client with buyer's remorse. Remember— logic and emotion.
> ➤ Never forget that you make the account list, not vice versa.
> ➤ Respond to opportunities in a timely fashion. When you are there first with the information, you set the tone for the opportunity. Then follow up and always attempt to be the last one in front of the decision-maker.
> ➤ The client owes us nothing. We must earn everything.

Volume #2 soon followed, titled, *Generating Added Value and Other Sales Tips to Ponder*. There were some similarities with volume #1. Sometimes looking for a different way of communicating the same message keeps the messaging fresh. If you haven't gotten tired of repeating your message, it probably hasn't begun to get traction with your team.

Like the earlier booklet, this *Generating Added Value* booklet enabled us to once again communicate to our staff and clients what we stood for in a somewhat entertaining, easy to understand fashion.

Volume 2: Generating Added Value and
Other Sales Tips to Ponder

➤ The person who complains about hard times and difficult business conditions and obstacles will rarely succeed during good times. The problem is in the "person" and not the times.

➤ Nothing great has ever been accomplished except by those who dared to believe the something inside if them was superior to circumstances. Prepare and work toward a goal, and it will likely be achieved.

➤ You usually get what you expect. If you believe your product is worth more, it will motivate you to go for a higher rate or share. If you believe your product is worth what the buyer is offering, you will accept what they give you. When you believe that the buyer is paying more for your product than you deserve, it will at some point sabotage your efforts.

➤ To establish maximum value, you must sell your prospect the way he/she is comfortable buying. Not the way you are comfortable selling. Be alert. Customize your approach.

➤ No problem can withstand the assault of sustained thinking and subsequent action. Sooner rather than later that one breakthrough strategy will reveal itself. Keep thinking and reflecting; the correct strategy or approach will become evident—often when and where you least expect it.

➤ Here is a story of four people who comprised the sales force of a once successful company. The salespeople's names were Everybody, Somebody, Anybody, and Nobody. There was an important job to be done, and Everybody was sure that Somebody would do it. Anybody could have done it, but Nobody did. Somebody got angry because it was Anybody's job. Everybody thought that Anybody could do it, but Nobody realized that Everybody wouldn't do it. It ended up that Everybody blamed Somebody when Nobody did what Anybody could have done. The moral is don't wait for Somebody, Anybody, or Everybody to do it. Do it yourself, and the sooner the better. Take action.

➤ One machine can do the work of ten ordinary people although no machine can do the work of one extraordinary person.

➤ When it appears as if you are no longer making progress with an account and you have run into a dead end, your next approach should come from an entirely different direction. Look at the facts backward, forward, and inside out. Question your assumptions and listen to your gut. Stand back, evaluate, and be flexible enough to alter your approach.

➤ The art of establishing maximum value is the art of knowing what facts and information to overlook. Identify what is truly important to your customers; if not, you will be wasting your time and theirs and forego making the sale.

➤ A problem well stated is a problem half-solved. Review your facts. Make sure you understand the real concern or objection. It is only then that you can begin to solve their problem. To get to this point, we must be active listeners— so few are.

➤ Do it now. Remember "one of these days" is never "one of these days."

➤ You get what you believe you deserve. The key is believing that your product deserves more and then acting on that belief. A buyer's conviction will usually match your conviction.

➤ You can close more business by becoming interested in other people and their success than by trying to get people interested in you or your product.

➢ Study the pricing tendencies and strategies of your competitors. People and companies are creatures of habit. Anticipate their tactics and be prepared to blunt their effectiveness.

➢ "Out-cheaping" the competition is here to stay. Elevate the negotiation from a discussion of efficiency to a discussion of value. Study and work at the art of negotiation.

➢ You need to "be" before you can "do," you have to "do" before you can "have." Continual improvement should be one of your paramount professional goals.

➢ Once you get the rate and share that you deserve, it is time for a quick celebration but not complacency. Next opportunity, try for more. Raise the bar.

➢ A tailor is a bright fellow. He takes a new measurement every time he sees one of his customers. Do not assume just because your client bought you once that they will forever more. Always be selling the value of your product. Good selling is never wasted. Assume your competition also believes this as well, and you won't be caught off guard.

➢ Presell as if your livelihood depended on it. In truth, it does.

➢ The greatest impediment to our success and self-improvement is that our demands on ourselves are so meager and few. The idea is not to just do enough to get by but to cheerfully chase excellence. Expect more of yourselves than others do. The difference between the possible and the impossible often lies in a seller's own determination. So, answer this question: What do you expect of yourself? Your long-term success depends on your answer.

➢ Provide "legendary" service. Service that is so good your customers brag about it. Are any clients bragging about what you have done for them lately? Business is like tennis— those that don't serve well, lose.

➢ It is impossible to establish the proper respect and appreciation for our product if we "don't know." Read books, take notes, review the notes, study the notes, ask questions, network, study the techniques of others, be inquisitive. Figuratively and literally, invest in your knowledge. It will be the best money you will ever spend. What percent of your income do you set aside for self-improvement? The best performers are and continue to be the best students throughout their careers.

➢ A successful seller rarely pegs his/her ability to get an order based on "price." He/she recognizes that they are the company's biggest competitive advantage. Computers, Arbitron numbers can't establish value, only effective salespeople can.

➢ Establishing value comes not from the spectacular but from the persistent pursuit of the mundane edge.

➢ Remember when you say you "can't" get a higher price make sure you are not saying that you "won't."

➢ Great sellers can always find a new sales point to highlight, even if it's an old one restated in a different manner. Be creative. Think of different ways of hammering home your sales story in new, compelling ways.

➢ A common mistake is taking a competitor's pricing strategy and packaging tactics as the standard by which to judge yours. Where is it written that your competitor is smarter or that their pricing is optimum? Where is it written that they know what you don't know?

➢ Those who are inclined to compromise too quickly can never establish value to the degree to which they might. Good judgement leads to higher shares and you can only acquire good judgement by reflecting upon your previous experiences and decisions.

➤ Look for ways to establish points of distinction. Many salespeople have lost their own points of distinction because they do nothing more than the minimum expected. A product sold in a "normal" way by a "normal" salesperson will develop a "normal" image and generate "normal" revenue, nothing special

➤ No one buys a product from a company. They buy it from a person. Someone they trust. Trust is to a relationship what oxygen is to surviving. Without trust, a meaningful business relationship can't survive.

➤ Getting a higher share and increased revenue depends on how you phrase your questions. Several groups of one hundred people were asked the following question. The first group was asked, "You don't want any apricots, do you?" 90 percent said no. The second group asked, "You do want apricots, don't you"? 50 percent said yes. The third group was asked, "Would you like one dish or two dishes of apricots?" 40 percent took two dishes and 50 percent took one dish. Don't underestimate the importance of correctly and effectively phrasing your questions and comments. Often, it is not what you say but how you say it.

➤ Look the buyer straight in the eye. State your price with conviction. Be proud of the price that you are quoting. Be proud of your product. Anticipate the buyer's reaction and be prepared. Sales is like chess. To succeed you must constantly be anticipating, thinking two or three steps ahead, putting yourself in a position to succeed.

➤ Most companies or individuals don't fail due to a lack of talent or strategic vision or lack of skills. They fail due to lack of execution. The boring execution of the little stuff. The stuff many of us don't think we need to do. The basic blocking and tackling that makes champions and championship teams.

➤ Don't limit your thinking to what "has been." Attempt to define "what should be" while preparing yourself for what "will be." Break out of the old paradigms to the new.

➤ It is the work that we do for our client that is not required that enables us to succeed. The person that cares the most typically will make the most money. The world is full of people who are willing to do all that is expected. The winners do a little bit more.

➤ Selling is like playing poker. It requires courage, intuition, and a healthy dose of common sense.

➤ Opt not to defend price but to explain value.

➤ There are usually two reasons for every action. The ones you are told and the real one. The great sellers can quickly see through this, identify the true objection, and then overcome it.

There was a third volume, which I could not locate, but while each took some time to compile; they did the trick and accomplished what they were designed to do—align our sales staff and to reconfirm to our clients our business philosophy.

What follows are some final elemental beliefs that have guided me over the years.

1. Just as a shark needs to keep moving forward to survive and thrive, the same is true for anyone in business who wants to succeed. It is grow or go.

2. It is time to consider a change of responsibilities if you stop getting butterflies. When the butterflies disappear, it is a sign that things are too comfortable, and outstanding accomplishments rarely come about by those in comfort.

3. Those who continue to grow are indefatigable in search of improvements, self and otherwise. Always strive to do everything a little better today than yesterday. Little by little

soon becomes a lot. Growth comes from daily incremental improvements, not from one massive growth spurt. Growth requires dissatisfaction with the status quo.

4. One's attitude and not aptitude determines the altitude. Talent is only a starting point. Attitude is more important than education and circumstances. It is more important than appearance, intelligence, and even skill. The right attitude enables one to meet the challenge and overcome chaos. Eradicate mental toxins that prevent you from accomplishing more.

5. You are completely in charge of your success or lack thereof. Success takes time. Be prepared for the long haul. Business is a marathon and not a sprint.

6. If you are not "fired" with enthusiasm, you will likely be "fired" with enthusiasm. Enthusiasm covers up mistakes and buys the time to rectify them.

7. The way to be safe is never be completely secure. Security is only imaginary. There is no security in nature, and there is certainly no security in business. We all require the spur of insecurity to be at our best.

8. Maintain a sense of urgency. If it is worth doing, it is worth being done with some urgency. Whenever I even walked to the men's room, I always walked with some urgency.

9. Refuse to accept the word *can't*. Eighteenth century writer Samuel Johnson aptly put it: "My dear friend, clear your mind of can't." Can't is all about limitations. Make sure you do not limit any of your success by believing in "can't."

Also, embrace the word *and* and forget the word *or*. *And* leads to promotions and excellence. *Or*, like the word *can't*, implies limitations and leads to mediocrity.

10. Embrace risk. Often not taking one is taking one. A turtle only makes progress when he sticks his neck out. Same with us.

11. Luck is for losers. Luck is more often than not the hardships and deprivations the successful have embraced and not hesitated to endure.

12. If you must deal in criticism, confine it to self-criticism. The most used "muscle" in business is the pointed finger. Point it toward yourself before pointing it at others.

13. If you are willing to ask dumb questions, you can learn anything. Just don't ask them twice.

14. Strive for perfection. Knowing it can't be achieved is no reason for not pursuing it. Life is like a ten-speed bike; most of us have gears we never use.

15. Always keep an open mind. The mind is like a parachute, functioning only when it is open. Avoid jumping to conclusions.

Everything in the preceding pages provides a solid blueprint to follow to be a leader and human being of significance. Borrow away and good luck!

ACKNOWLEDGMENTS

Much of what I have accomplished in sports and business I have accomplished largely due to the lessons taught to me by my father. He was an amazing man. My mom, a beautiful woman, passed away too soon. Two months prior to Mom's passing, my dad after twenty-five years left a salary job at New York Life for a 100 percent commission sales position. He worked his tail off under very difficult circumstances to support and raise three kids under fourteen.

My mentors, whom I referenced earlier in this book, were also instrumental and had a huge impact on my life and career. I honestly have no clue where I would be today had John Picirrillo not taken a chance on me in Richmond. He set the tone for my career. In retrospect, each one of my previous bosses had one thing in common— ironclad integrity. My best pal, Rich Roper, spent countless hours with me on the court challenging me to get better every step of the way at May Moore school, often fouling the hell out of me along the way. My brother Steve was also a great influence throughout high school and college. Not many guys get to play with their brother on the same college basketball team. The only problem was he rarely passed me the ball. Kevin Eastman, who did pass me the ball, has remained a good friend. Mitch Kupchak, who taught me about the importance of attitude and the UNC way, has as well. Stu Olds was amazing. Mike Agovino, Evan Greenberg, Bob

Turner, Steven Moskowitz, Erik Hellum, and Peter Burton became lifelong friends, as have many, many others. I am blessed.

Of course, there are my kids, Meagan, Michael, Ashley, and Sean, and three step kids, Margaret, Will, and Charlie, who all put up with my lectures about hustle and excellence. They had no choice. Then, there is my glorious wife, Sydney. She came into my life at the lowest of points and elevated me every step of the way for the past twenty years. I would probably be in a cave now if it were not for her. She is a saint, and I could not love her any more than I do. Finally, there are the grandkids, Cami, Taylor, Tristan, Olivia, Scarlett, Andrew, Dylan, and Sienna, all wonderful young people!

Writing this book has been a very pleasant experience reminiscing about all the terrific people I had the privilege of working for and with during my career who have enriched my life immeasurably. These folks universally were dedicated, principled professionals who understood the importance of hard work, possessed integrity, and embraced winning the right way, elevating me, as I hope I was able to elevate them.

I would like to thank these other folks for also positively impacting me along the way. Alphabetically: Jill Albert, Richie Balsbaugh, Caroline Beasley, Bruce Beasley, Brian Beasley, Josh Becker, Brian Benedik, Gerry Boehme, Carl Butrum, Bob Case, Mike Chires, Charlie Columbo, Cheryl Cooper, Glen Corneliess, Elissa DiDonato, Steve Dodge, Bill Fortenbaugh, Dan Frisbie, Peter Gardner, Greg Glenday, Liz Haban, John Hogan, Jeff Howard, Don Jacobs, Larry Julius, Mitch Kline, Alan Korowitz, Jamie Kriegel, Kevin LeGrett, Bob Liodice, Milt McConnel, Jay McCurdy, Cindy McCurdy, Brian McElroy, Bill McElveen, Mary Menna, Steve Meyers, Dom Milano, Lew Mills, Heather Monahan, Mike Moran, Paul Murray, Bob Pittman, Bonnie Press, Bob Proffitt, Charlie Rahilly, Bruce Reese, Larry Roberts, Ruth Roman, John Scanlon, Tom Schurr, Danielle Sledge, Carl Slone, and Jeff Warshaw.

AFTERWORD

On July 29, 2020, my husband, Bob, lost his hard-fought battle with cancer. For two and a half years he endured rounds of chemo, radiation, and a grueling surgery, yet he continued to find joy in his work through it all. Every day, he was a craftsman at his desk, creating ways to help colleagues in his field across the country. His focus was excellence. He amazed me with his determination, his will, and his positive attitude. We were hopeful his cure was just around the corner until we understood that was not to be. This bonded us together on a road of shared courage.

Bob McCurdy was a steady and constant student. He read all there was to know about advertising, his clients' businesses, and industry trends. Then he read it again. Bob devoted many weekend hours to research so he could be "better on Monday." If we went to the beach on a Saturday, he brought business trades, articles, and his famous yellow highlighter, instead of a novel. His quest for knowledge was contagious for those around him, including me. As serious as he was about his work—flying to LA or driving to Boston or catching the 4:50 a.m. train to New York—he had a soft side and a wonderful sense of humor. He made us laugh, and he also laughed at himself. He and I felt blessed to have found each other. When we met twenty years ago, we said, "Forty more." He left our world way too early. The extent to which he is missed by me and our family is immeasurable.

Bob often talked about writing a book someday. He had saved

countless boxes of notes, emails, and memos from his long career, and he felt he had a good story to tell. As we moved from house to house, the boxes followed us. In late December 2019, Bob finally began putting all his thoughts on paper, working on *The Quest for Excellence* over the long holiday week, ten hours a day. When he retired in April, he devoted each day to writing, hoping his insights and leadership skills could help his colleagues in their own quest for excellence. He had always known what the format would be and was excited when it started coming together. Finishing this book was the last great joy of Bob's career but not of his life. *That* was being Pop Pop to our eight grandchildren.

—Sydney McCurdy

Bob was racing against the clock to complete *The Quest* ... during his last year of life. Like he always did, he found a way to complete the job regardless of the adversity he faced. I think it was so important to him because he knew what a gift the book could be to so many. There's never been a better coach than Bob.

He understood that the essence of leadership is casting a vision worthy of the chase, chasing that vision side by side with your team (not from a corner office), deriving satisfaction from the achievements/growth of your people, accepting the responsibility for failures, and welcoming the burden of honesty in your communication. He lived these things every day of his life.

My heart is broken, my friend and mentor is gone, but I'm grateful to him for leaving us all this great remembrance. This book is Bob, and I'll cherish it always.

—Mike Agovino
President/CEO
Workhouse Connect LLC

At some point in time those who have had some success in business take pause to reflect about what got them to where they are. What or who influenced them in some profound way ? In my case the "who" was Bob McCurdy. From the very first day I met Bob, I felt his energy, intelligence, power, and drive, but most importantly his personal interest in helping me become great.

Bob was a natural leader. He became my coach, cheerleader, and forever mentor. He taught me why preparation was so critical for success, why energy and passion made a difference, and what it really meant to "show up." His motto, "fail to prepare or prepare to fail," became my own. I was lucky enough to have worked for Bob and then continued a thirty-year friendship.

I will miss our frequent breakfasts and lunches discussing life and business; but I'm thrilled that Bob was able to finish *The Quest for Excellence*. Right up until the end, Bob continued to focus on inspiring others through his own life lessons.

Thanks again, Bob. You have left a legacy that will live on.

—Evan Greenberg
CEO
allscopeMEDIA

Bob was a larger than life leader, manager, and coach. His enthusiasm and drive to "be the best" was contagious and only eclipsed by his intense focus on developing people to reach their maximum potential.

I joined the McCurdy team in '85, and over the course of a number of years he helped define my skills and enhance my productivity as a manager and leader. What separated Bob from other business teachers were his unwavering expectations. He expected you to dedicate yourself to the mastery of the basics (his ideas of what it takes to achieve excellent outcomes), leading by example at every decision intersection, and staying the course when developing a diverse group of learners. Giving endless energy to preparation, having total familiarity with products and industries, and going the extra mile for customers and colleagues are tenets he preached. I credit much of my career success to Bob's early lessons and continued advice as a mentor and friend over thirty-five years.

It is exhilarating to know that Bob's leadership wisdom will continue through this book for future generations of rising stars in business who have an appetite to learn and gain a competitive advantage to win.

—Steven Moskowitz, President and CEO, Centennial Towers Holding, LP

Many have a desire to leave their mark on the world once they're gone. So few are able to do so. For those that are able to accomplish this, they are never really gone, as their legacy lives on through those that they have touched throughout their lives.

Bob made everyone around him better. His habits became your habits, his expectations became your expectations, and his relentless pursuit of victory became your relentless pursuit of victory. He hated losing more than he liked winning. What has stuck more than anything with me over the years is the importance of preparation. His lessons have helped carry me through a successful thirty-year career.

In this book you'll witness how a true overachiever operates. If you want to improve your leadership skills and your approach to winning in business and in life, this book is a must read.

Bob left his mark on me and his spirit will remain always in my thoughts and with my actions.

—Peter Burton
VP/market manager
Beasley/Las Vegas

Bob and I we were teammates in college at the University of Richmond. During that time, he gave me my first master class on the power of continuous learning, developing, understanding, and curiosity. Little did he know it at the time, but I believe the title of his book began back then as he lived *The Quest for Excellence* every day.

There are those times in life when people and wisdom walk into your life, and they impact your life without you even knowing it. As Bob and I worked on our basketball skills every day in the heat of the gym and away from the bright lights of the game night arena, he provided a walking example of "what you do behind the scenes is what prepares for when you are in front of the crowds on game night." He taught me that it's much more about what you do than it is about what you talk about doing. As I look back on it now, he was mentoring even before he got in the corporate world and mentored so many.

As I read his book, I knew it would be filled with pearls of wisdom. So, if you are looking for a book that will give you a game plan for success, challenge you to become your best, and give you immediate and actionable strategies that you can insert into your job, career, or life, this book does this and much more. It is a must read if you are looking to take that next step.

I saw all of these principles pay off firsthand as I spent two years with Bob in the ever-competitive world of college basketball.

—Kevin Eastman
Former NBA championship coach—Boston Celtics
Current corporate and sports team speaker

Bob McCurdy was a good friend and longtime business associate who was one of the most successful and competitive sales executives I ever met.

What you will learn in this book is the art of sales from a true champion of the sport. *The Quest for Excellence* delivers a unique perspective from an executive who consistently delivered the goods across thousands of career sales wins. He also taught hundreds of others how to do the same.

Where else are you going to read a book on success-based thinking written by the 1975 leading scorer in Men's Division 1 NCAA basketball. Enjoy reading *The Quest for Excellence*.

—Dave Crowl
Regional vice president/market manager
Cumulus Radio Station Group-Cincinnati, Ohio

I first met Bob McCurdy some thirty-six years ago. I was interviewing with him for a sales position at KATZ Radio in New York. Bob's interview process was grueling. The more difficult he made it, the more I realized how badly I wanted to work under him. They say you appreciate most what you work hardest for, and I knew Bob would push me harder and prepare me better for success than anyone else in media.

I'm very proud of the fact that I became Bob's first hire in the New York office, in September 1984.

I have never met anyone like Bob, and I owe a great deal to him. He was my mentor, trainer, and coach during the formative years of my career. Bob was the critical player in my growth, enabling me to become president of multiple radio representation companies and enjoy a successful career. For thirty-six years, Bob has been my mentor, teammate, competitor, and friend.

I didn't know it at the time, but our last get-together was a lunch at the Westport diner. We spent three hours reminiscing, laughing, and crying—all happy tears. I was able to share with Bob that day all that he had meant to me. I'll always remember the look of pride on his face as I thanked him for being such a powerful force in my life.

I'm confident that anyone who reads this book will absorb some of that same power Bob McCurdy gave me.

—Bob Turner
President Sales, Azteca Television

I was fortunate to have known Bob for over twenty-five years as a boss, friend, coach, mentor, and teacher. Over the years, Bob influenced and built countless careers, and many of us are filled with both gratitude and admiration. His work ethic, attention to detail, passion for learning, and high expectations were noteworthy, but what stands out the most to me was his acute ability to truly *listen* to others. In an age where everyone loves to talk, Bob possessed a unique ability to understand your point of view.

I have enjoyed a fruitful audio career with leadership roles across radio, early days digital audio, and most recently streaming audio on a global scale building Spotify. The constant educating and coaching from Bob have undoubtedly made me better, and I have always tried to pay it forward to the people on my teams.

This book is a hands-on compilation of sales tactics and leadership teachings, but more importantly it's a road map on how to live a fruitful and successful life.

—Brian Benedik
Former Spotify Global chief revenue officer

I have always enjoyed reading, listening, and debating anything Bob McCurdy decided to share with me. Each experience offered an opportunity to alter my perspective and expand my knowledge.

He truly transformed my approach to marketing through teaching a game plan for success.

The Quest for Excellence is no different. Bob draws from his vast experiences and relationships to deliver a powerful narrative. His message is not only relevant in business but carries over to our daily lives.

—Kevin LeGrett
President, iHeartMedia

I was well into my forty-plus-year career when I finally had the pleasure and honor of meeting Bob. As we spent time together, my respect and appreciation for him grew. His depth of knowledge and passion for the business are unrivaled. Bob became a mentor to me both personally and professionally.

One of the many traits I admired about Bob was his willingness to devote time to help anyone who had an interest in learning. He did not discriminate; if someone was willing to put the work into learning, Bob was ready to put his time into teaching that person.

I grew to have great respect for Bob, and I'm grateful that we became close friends. I look forward to passing on many of his pearls of wisdom. This book is a treasure chest full of the best of Bob.

—Brian Beasley
EVP/chief operating officer
Beasley Media Group

If there were an all-time fantasy league for coaches, Bob would have been everyone's first pick. But he was so much more than just a supreme coach, teacher, and leader; he was a gift to the teams he built and led and to the business world itself.

Bob's unique ability to mold a group of people into a team with a common goal was legendary. He understood the critical mission of focusing on the fundamentals almost obsessively—and the virtual surety that success would follow.

Spending time with Bob always left me feeling a little bit smarter, considerably more optimistic about our business, and grateful to have a friend who was such a remarkable coach and mentor.

I will miss him forever but am thankful that he left us with *The Quest for Excellence*.

—Bill McElveen, regional president and chief compliance officer, Alpha Media

ABOUT THE AUTHOR

I spent forty-four years on the sales side of the radio business. The first four locally in Richmond, Virginia, (WLEE AM) and Indianapolis, Indiana, (WNDE/WFBQ) where I rose from account executive to local sales manager. The next thirty-four years on the national side as an account executive, sales manager, general sales manager, and president. As president, I ran Katz Radio for six years, started Sentry and Amcast, both national radio sales firms, building each from the ground up and was co-president of Clear Channel Radio Sales (CCRS). After CCRS, I transferred over to run Katz Marketing Solutions (KMS) as its president, which was a unit dedicated to developing new radio dollars at the senior levels of both agency and advertiser. After KMS, I consulted Alpha Broadcasting and the Beasley Media Group for two years before joining Beasley full time in 2016. I retired in April 2020.

Radio has been not only my profession but my hobby as well. I have been extremely fortunate to have this be the case, although it did not happen by accident; it first requires a commitment. If one makes a profound commitment, fervent passion usually follows. That is when it is possible for a profession to make the transition to hobby.

CPSIA information can be obtained
at www.ICGtesting.com
Printed in the USA
LVHW031729041021
699496LV00005B/123

9 781665 702775